DMU 0330563 01 4

AF750517

PUNISHING CRIMINALS

Recent Titles in
Contributions in Criminology and Penology

Chinese Subculture and Criminality: Non-traditional Crime Groups in America
Ko-lin Chin

A Sword for the Convicted: Representing Indigent Defendants on Appeal
David T. Wasserman

Delinquency in Puerto Rico: The 1970 Birth Cohort Study
Dora Nevares, Marvin E. Wolfgang, and Paul E. Tracy with the Collaboration of Steven Aurand

Waging the Battle Against Drunk Driving: Issues, Countermeasures, and Effectiveness
Gerald D. Robin

Policing Western Europe: Politics, Professionalism, and Public Order, 1850–1940
Clive Emsley and Barbara Weinberger, editors

Policing a Socialist Society: The German Democratic Republic
Nancy Travis Wolfe

Domestic Marijuana: A Neglected Industry
Ralph A. Weisheit

Personality and Peer Influence in Juvenile Corrections
Martin Gold and D. Wayne Osgood

Bad Guys and Good Guys: Moral Polarization and Crime
Daniel S. Claster

Innovative Approaches in the Treatment of Drug Abuse: Program Models and Strategies
James A. Inciardi, Frank M. Tims, and Bennett W. Fletcher, editors

Coca and Cocaine: An Andean Perspective
Felipe E. MacGregor, editor

Police Under Pressure: Resolving Disputes
Robert Coulson

4SA

WITHDRAWN
DE MONTFORT UNIVERSITY
LIBRARY

PUNISHING CRIMINALS

Developing Community-Based Intermediate Sanctions

MALCOLM DAVIES

Contributions in Criminology and Penology, Number 41
MARVIN WOLFGANG, *Series Adviser*

GREENWOOD PRESS
Westport, Connecticut • London

DE MONTFORT UNIVERSITY
LIBRARY
Acc. No.
Date -5 FEB 1996
Loc./Form
Class 364.68
DAV

Library of Congress Cataloging-in-Publication Data

Davies, Malcolm.
Punishing criminals : developing community-based intermediate sanctions / Malcolm Davies.
p. cm.—(Contributions in criminology and penology, ISSN 0732-4464 ; no. 41)
Includes bibliographical references and index.
ISBN 0-313-28033-9 (alk. paper)
1. Community-based corrections—California—Public opinion.
2. Criminal justice, Administration of—California—Public opinion.
3. Punishment—California—Public opinion. 4. Public opinion—California. 5. Criminal justice personnel—California—Attitudes.
I. Title. II. Series.
HV9279.D38 1993
364.6′8—dc20 93-9315

British Library Cataloguing in Publication Data is available.

Copyright © 1993 by Malcolm Davies

All rights reserved. No portion of this book may be reproduced, by any process or technique, without the express written consent of the publisher.

Library of Congress Catalog Card Number: 93-9315
ISBN: 0-313-28033-9
ISSN: 0732-4464

First published in 1993

Greenwood Press, 88 Post Road West, Westport, CT 06881
An imprint of Greenwood Publishing Group, Inc.

Printed in the United States of America

The paper used in this book complies with the Permanent Paper Standard issued by the National Information Standards Organization (Z39.48-1984).

10 9 8 7 6 5 4 3 2 1

Copyright Acknowledgments

The author and the publisher are grateful to the following for granting the use of material:

A. P. Cohen, *The Symbolic Construction of Community*. 1989. London: Routledge.

D. Stewart and P. Shamdasini, *Focus Groups: Theory and Practice*. 1990. Reprinted by permission of Sage Publications, Inc.

In addition, the author wishes to thank the California Department of Justice for their permission to quote from the following publications:

Davies, M. (1988) *Survey Report: The Expansion of the Criminal Justice and Penal System in California—Is Greater Coordination Required?*, Bureau of Criminal Statistics Monograph Series, Sacramento: Office of the Attorney General, California Department of Justice.

Davies, M. (1988) *Coordinating Justice in California: There Ought To Be a Law About It*, Bureau of Criminal Statistics Forum Series, Sacramento: Office of the Attorney General, California Department of Justice.

Davies, M. (1992) *A Policy Role for Focus Groups: Community Corrections*, Bureau of Criminal Statistics Forum Series, Sacramento: California Department of Justice.

This book is dedicated to John Conrad (1913–1992)
criminologist and penal reformer

Contents

Acknowledgments

I would like to thank my colleagues, family, friends, research assistants, officials, and backers who encouraged and supported my research in California.

This includes those responsible for the California Attorney General's Senior Research Fellowship program, which allowed me to engage in an uninterrupted year of research in California at the Bureau of Criminal Statistics in Sacramento, and who provided the administrative support for the survey and focus group inquiry.

Financial support also came from the Guggenheim Criminal Justice program at Berkeley, and the Nuffield Foundation, London. Academic and administrative backing came from the Faculty at the Center for the Study of Law and Society, Berkeley, where I was a visiting scholar from 1987 to 1988 and in 1990. I was made most welcome and provided with administrative assistance by the Law Faculty at the University of California, Davis while I was a visiting scholar (1987–1988 and 1990). Encouragement, advice, and useful contacts came from the Presley Institute, California.

There are many individuals to whom I owe gratitude. They include from the Bureau of Criminal Statistics, California Department of Justice in Sacramento: Shirley Anderson, Michelle

Azevedo, Claudia Ball, Rebecca Bowe, Michelle Dille, Quint Hegner, Ron Lai, Ted Olsen, and Bill Whitney.

A number of California county criminal justice officials helped to ensure the successful completion of my research. I offer my thanks to Bob Cushman (Santa Clara County Executive Office), Dick Foreman (Los Angeles County Sheriff's Department), Bob Kelgord (Sacramento County Probation Department), Barry Nidorf (Los Angeles County Probation Department), Ron Obert (Office of Pre-Trial Services, Santa Clara), John Pearson (Napa County Department of Corrections), Richard Rainey (Sheriff, Contra Costa County), and Gary Tatum (Police Chief, Vacaville).

In Sacramento I received welcome advice from Bob Dickover and Greg Harding (California Department of Corrections), Elaine Duxbury (California Youth Authority), Suzie Cohen (California Probation, Parole and Correctional Association), Bob Holmes (Senator Presley's Office in the Legislature), Senator Robert Presley, and James Park.

A number of academics, practitioners, colleagues, and friends have helped over the years to shape my thoughts about the topics and themes discussed in this book and I wish to thank them. They are John Conrad (who died during the completion of this manuscript in October 1992), Malcolm Feeley (Berkeley), Floyd Feeney (UC, Davis), David Garland (Edinburgh University), Sheldon Messinger (Berkeley), Ken Plummer (Essex University), Jim Rasmussen (Bureau of Criminal Statistics, Sacramento), Brian Taugher (Attorney General's office, Sacramento), Nigel Walker (Cambridge University), and Clive Welsh (Prison Service, United Kingdom).

Academics and former colleagues have assisted by their comments, advice, and support over many years. I owe thanks to Jo Borril, Dean Clark, Hazel Croall, Barry King, Nigel Fielding, Dave Glen, Michael Molyneux, Leslie Sheinman, Jane Tyrer, and Frank Webster.

In the production of the manuscript I was helped, crucially at times, by Rick Burne and Robert Stockton from the Telecom Capita Computer Service at Thames Valley University.

For the detailed and diplomatic task of sub-editing the manuscript I owe a great deal to Vivien Fraser, Alex Weich, and Tony Roberts.

Finally, I must thank two people who have worked in support of this project in a most professional, dedicated and tireless way: Saralee Buck from the Law School, UC Davis; and Michele Rose from the Bureau of Criminal Statistics, Office of the Attorney General, California.

Professor Malcolm Davies

Abbreviations

BCS	Bureau of Criminal Statistics, California Department of Justice
BRC	Blue Ribbon Commission, California
CCPOA	California Correctional and Peace Officers Association
CDC	California Department of Corrections
CPPCA	California Probation, Parole and Correctional Association
CYA	California Youth Authority
NACRO	National Association for the Care and Resettlement of Offenders, United Kingdom

Introduction

Could we punish criminals without sending them to prison? This question was to become the key to policy discussions in the 1990s as sentencing and correctional authorities went in search of community-based forms of intermediate sanctions.

Some penal reformers have answered this question from the viewpoint that prisons and the idea of punishment is an unworthy aspect of a civilized society, others from the perspective that prisons do little to change the future behavior of incarcerated offenders. I take the view that, although the purposes of sentencing are many, the penal system is not to be judged exclusively from an individual offender perspective; a community-oriented approach to punishment requires an understanding of the public's response to crime. This is especially important at a time when ever-increasing exhortations are being made to make less use of imprisonment and keep an ever larger number of offenders in the communities in which they have been convicted of committing criminal offenses.

Would the idea that criminals could be punished without sending them to prison be acceptable to the public? A move toward the greater use of community-based intermediate sanctions would require penal reformers and policy makers to focus their attention on the issue of public and professional confidence in community sanctions.

Much of the funded research effort to date has been directed at the impact of intermediate sanctions on individual offenders and whether intermediate sanctions work to reduce criminality. Too little attention has been given as to how intermediate sanctions could achieve credibility among the public and criminal justice officials. Hence, the need to supplement effectiveness-evaluation studies with the evaluation of confidence in different forms of community sanctions.

The rationale given for extending the use of community sanctions is based on a combination of fiscal costs and the ineffectiveness of prisons in deterring or rehabilitating individual offenders. But the awareness that prisons have failed to deter or rehabilitate those sent to these costly institutions provides a reason for making less use of prisons. It does not offer a rationale for intermediate sanctions. Furthermore, the offender-oriented perspectives provided by rehabilitative and deterrent theorists do not take into account the impact on the community of punishment through imprisonment.

A more community-oriented theory of punishment would need to evaluate the effectiveness of the impact of penal sanctions on the public's confidence in the criminal justice system. The community's concern about crime provides a better starting point for a theory of punishment, if penal policy is to successfully address the problem of the public's fear of crime and its confidence in the criminal justice system. A synthesis of denunciatory and retributive principles provides an acceptable rationale for the criminal justice system.

Thus I argue for the need to develop the insights of theories that relate punishment to community in a way that gives conceptual priority to the community and its values, rather than to criminals and their behavior. In seeking to answer the question of whether punishment without imprisonment is both feasible and credible, I have invoked theoretical insights from penology, policy studies, politics, and sociology; and I have set forth a rationale for intermediate sanctions from a denunciatory-retributive perspective.

Empirical information is provided by two studies of senior criminal justice officials in California. This information is based on research I carried out in 1988 and 1990, with the cooperation of the California Attorney General's office in Sacramento and the Law School, University of California at Davis. The first study was a survey about the impact of the expansion throughout the 1980s. The second investigation used focus groups to assess the views of criminal justice officials about the extension of community sanctions to a wider range of offenders. The results of the latter study were set out in a report to the California Legislature at a special legislative hearing on the future of community corrections.

These two empirical investigations led me to the conclusion that there is need for an improved process of consultation between policy makers, officials, and the public to ascertain views about acceptable forms of punishment in the community. Ironically, there are radical penal reformers who shun the idea of public contribution to policy debate in this field. They fear the public's reaction. My fear was that the simplistic way penal policy had been presented to the public in the past would continue to result in troublesome polarizations. In an attempt to improve this situation, I have explored the use of focus groups as a method of consultation.

There exist many variations of community-based sentencing sanctions across the United States. Much professional experience in dealing with offenders in the community and a strong fiscal and penological rationale for making less use of imprisonment are evident as well. What is lacking is a convincing case for community-based intermediate sanctions.

PUNISHMENT WITHOUT IMPRISONMENT?

Inspired by the belief that prisons are costly and inhumane institutions that do little good, the prison reductionists seem to have won the argument in the United States. Previous attempts to introduce alternatives to imprisonment were derived from the assumptions of the prison reductionists and those committed to rehabilitation and a view that prisons were inhumane and uncivilized. They assume the overuse of imprisonment, an assumption justified by contrasting incarceration rates from around the world. These show the United States with a rate three times that of the United Kingdom, and the United Kingdom at the top of the European league table of prison users.

From the prison reductionist perspective, it was correct to talk of alternatives to prison—as that was the goal—to reduce the use of custody. It was reformers with this perspective who spearheaded the "alternatives" movement. The corollary to these assumptions was that sentencing should be about "positive" and "constructive" approaches toward the offender. Hence, the early alternatives were both inspired and blinkered by a rehabilitative logic, which was presented as both more humane and constructive.

This viewpoint has now changed. In January 1990, a watershed year in California, the Blue Ribbon Commission's Report "Inmate Population Management" was published. This publication showed that the hunt was on for a secondary sanction, which would not replace imprisonment, but would provide an additional step in the hierarchy of penalties available to the courts. These would operate as an intermediate form of punishment. The reports targeted prison-bound inmate populations, focusing on property offenders, and effectively highlighted the issue of what to do with persistent property and drug related offenders if they are not to be sent to prison. The report stressed the need for alternatives that could be regarded as non-prison forms of punishment. While recognizing the failure of prisons in terms of deterrence and rehabilitative criteria, prisons would still play a major role when handling violent and serious offenders either for the purpose of punishment or public protection. But what can be done with prison-bound offenders, now that incarceration has become too costly and unfashionable with policy makers? However, the question, "What works?" has to be set alongside the question, "What is acceptable?" Crime figures continue to rise, inspiring a high level of fear among the public and an anxiety about their safety in those very communities to which these policy makers would now return ever more convicted criminals.

If intermediate sanctions are to be effective and acceptable, more thought must be given to the justification of the role to be played by intermediate sanctions, and how this should be related to the multiple goals that a criminal justice system aspires to achieve. Furthermore, much of the analysis of the impact of sentencing stresses the importance of cost-effectiveness and underestimates the significance of the community's confidence in different forms of punishment.

DEVELOPMENTS IN PENAL POLICY IN CALIFORNIA

Has the era of unbridled prison construction been played out in California? A move toward less reliance on prisons and an increase in the use of community-based intermediate sanctions was a key recommendation of the Blue Ribbon Commission Report produced in Sacramento in 1990.

The Deukmejian era in California (1982–1990), relied on a strong approach to "law and order." Governor Deukmejian campaigned heavily on "getting tough on crime." His administration oversaw an expanded and better resourced criminal justice system. He had inherited a prison system in which there had been very little spent on prison building. In 1982 no new prisons had been built for twenty years.

In California there were twelve state prisons in 1982. Since then twelve more have been built, resulting in a total expansion of 37,300 beds. This cost $3.2 billion to build and even more to operate. In addition, 40,764 new jail beds have been built by local governments for detaining defendants awaiting trial and for holding short-term commitments.

The number of state prison inmates in California has risen in a decade from 24,000 in 1980 to 90,000 in 1990. The budget of the Department of Corrections in California continued to grow faster than that of any other government department. The future operating costs of the expanded penal estate in California have not gone unnoticed. The cost of running the state prisons rose from $419 million in 1981 to $1.7 billion in 1989. By 1992 the average yearly cost of keeping a person in prison in California was $20,908 (CDC Facts, 1992, p. 1).

The Blue Ribbon Commission Report signified that the prison boom in California was coming to an end. That is not to imply that prisons will not be needed or built in the future. If they are, it is unlikely that so many will be built in so concentrated a period of time as we witnessed in the 1980s.

SENTENCING POLICY: THE SEARCH FOR INTERMEDIATE SANCTIONS

Community corrections is the flavor of the month in penological circles. Across the United States, policy makers have indicated the need to put a new emphasis on that timeworn concern of what to do with the throngs of prisoners and potential prisoners who fill the prisons to near capacity. The disillusionment, which twenty years ago was associated with rehabilitation and its failure to deliver the goods, is now extended to the 1980s era of penal expansion. The new prison buildings and enlarged penal populations have not noticeably reduced crime (the California Crime Index fell between 1980 and 1984, then increased up to 1990). The cost of this expansion will fall on future generations of taxpayers, who will have to pay the ever-increasing cost of operating the prisons.

Hence the search theoretically for intermediate sanctions and at the policy level for new versions of community corrections. Since the 1960s we have had a procession of innovations aimed at keeping offenders out of prisons (i.e., diversion, alternatives to custody, community service, etc.). They failed to stem the tide of rising criminality, as measured by official police statistics and crime surveys. They failed to stem the numbers going through a steadily growing penal process. They failed to convince the public and many of the professional groups involved in the criminal justice process that they were appropriate punishments for serious and persistent offenders.

They lacked credibility, partly because they were seen to be introduced to combat the spiraling costs of imprisonment. This encouraged cynicism. Furthermore, the moral entrepreneurs of such schemes were depicted as being soft on crime and as believing in an ideology that considered rehabilitation as the main goal of the penal system. Hence community-based sentencing innovations were introduced with a rehabilitative logic dressed up with a fiscal rationale.

If a new era of community corrections is to be introduced, it must have credibility with more groups than the probation and social worker professionals whose legitimate professional concern is with rehabilitation. However, rehabilitation is not the only goal of a criminal justice and penal system, and it is my contention that it is not the primary goal of the system.

Unfortunately, much of the theoretical and policy development work on community-based sanctions has been and is being done by those imbued, professionally and ideologically, with a rehabilitative fix. Those who adopted this orientation to punishment find it difficult to recognize that prisons are regarded as an acceptable form of punishment by the public and by sentencers. This is the dilemma for those proposing alternatives to prison. Anthony Vass declared in the preface to his *Alternatives to Prison*:

> I believe that prisons are bad; that there are better, more acceptable ways of punishing and controlling offenders than sending them to prison. Community alternatives—whether one calls them alternatives to custody, or supervision, or punishment in the community—provide a reasonable and, as will be shown, equally "effective" way of administering penalties against people who commit criminal offenses. In a sense I am making a moral judgement here. The moral issue is that alternatives are a more desirable approach to punishing offenders, if that is what it is all about, than locking them up in conditions which are an affront to a society which is called "civilized."(Vass, 1990, p. xi)

Vass makes it quite clear that it is not just prison conditions that are an affront to a civilized society, but the idea of prisons. Whether Vass is correct to assume that community sanctions are "equally effective" as prisons is an issue requiring a more sophisticated evaluation than Vass allows for, as one vital aspect of effectiveness is the community's confidence in community penalties. And while some prison conditions are an affront to civilized standards, many are not. The crux of the argument lies not in asserting the uncivilized aspect of imprisonment, but in finding non-prison forms of sanctions that inspire confidence and are acceptable to the public.

Much of the literature shuns the issue of acceptability and public confidence in forms of punishment. Too often the orthodox research establishment encourages a focus exclusively on effectiveness as interpreted to mean the impact on the offender's current and future criminal activities, as measured by recidivism rates. Hence, effectiveness is defined exclusively in terms of the impact on offenders as measured by comparative numerical data.

Major shifts in the penological paradigm are not achieved through studies of effectiveness, but through the redefinitions of what is an acceptable form of punishment to the community, within the practical constraints of the administration and funding of the criminal justice system. An equally important part of the penal balance is the impact that punishment has on the wider community of citizens.

If community corrections are to gain wider public acceptance, they have to escape the polarized image of being a "soft" form of sanction, in contrast to the "hard" impression that prisons have among the public and sentencers. Hence, the search for an intermediate sanction that would have public acquiescence—that would be considered more demanding than routine community-based sentencing options but less harsh than incarceration.

COMMUNITY AND PUNISHMENT

The idea of community has had mixed fortunes in penological and sociological debate. Misleadingly, it has come to mean since the 1960s any place other than an expensive institution paid for by the public. Or, it is a place where pressure groups describe their potential recruits as being at risk, for example, women or minority groups. Commercial interests have reinforced the view that the community is a threatening and unsafe place. In the meantime, the sale of alarms, lights, and grills grows. In sociological research the idea of community has suffered even more. Conflict-driven interpreters of society have found community to exist only among the socially marginal, the poor, and oppressed.

Community can exist on a larger scale, if we understand the Durkheimian concern with shared values as the defining reality of communities. My orientation is premised on the views of Thomas Hobbes and Emile Durkheim: we cannot take social order for granted, and the first concern of a criminal justice system is the maintenance of order in the community. This is achieved directly, at times through the coercive arm of the law, but also indirectly through the consequences for public morality of the community-level debates inspired by crime and our response to it. Public morality is not a fixed object but requires continual redefinition. The social construction of morality is inevitably bound up in the social processes by which we come to define and identify people as antisocial. The special form of regulatory norms we use to do this, the criminal law, is inevitably linked to our perceptions and moral interpretations of current, concrete events, circumstances, and behavior. The business of the criminal law is just one, albeit conspicuous, thread in the tapestry of public morality.

THEORY AND PENAL POLICY

Despite our extensive knowledge of human behavior and misbehavior, we have not found a solution to the problem of crime. The creation of more theories may have added to the problem by encouraging unrealizable public expectations. New theories are presented to the naive as a panacea. More seasoned observers note that the pendulum swings between allocating blame to the individual or to society. Our understanding of crime is still partial and limited and our responses to it are simplified into poorly framed policy choices.

I do not exclude the contribution of sociologists when I say that many of the responses to policy issues in penology have been unnecessarily polarized, for example, the posturing around "soft" versus "hard," "left" versus "right," or the tendency to adopt one purpose of punishment from the standpoint of professional interests. The end result of this style of debate is to reduce penal policy-making to nothing more than political slogans.

Nor are the politicians excused for unrealistically raising public expectations, by the pretense that they could or can solve crime. The 1968 and 1972 presidential election campaigns to elect Richard Nixon and Spiro Agnew set new heights in exploiting the public's anxiety about law and order.

The purposes of criminal policy are many and the balance depends on the extent and nature of crime, the complexities of society, and how those complexities are represented and resolved.

We do not need to add to this already oversimplistic view of crime and its solution, yet more academic tracts that are blinkered by the theoretical assumptions of their progenitors. We should be sensitized, not dominated, by the insights that past theoreticians have provided. An approach based on the perspectives of the sociology of law can be helpful in understanding penal policy if we keep in mind the fact that they are perspectives that not only provide us with a way of seeing the world, but also blind us to other aspects of the world.

Academic theories can be misleading in two ways. First, they inevitably simplify the world by classifying it into conceptual parcels that are readily understood. How one moves toward a relatively more accurate appreciation and interpretation of the social world should be the main business of academics in the social sciences. Second, theory is often a substitute for empirical inquiry. The question of whether policy decisions are the product of a manipulative elite operating in its self or class interest is a question of empirical assessment rather than preconceived assertion. For some commentators on penal affairs, the theory is more important than the phenomena being discussed. Such theory-blinded analysis is akin to religion, and stances are taken regardless of evidence. I can do little to persuade those who abuse the academic tradition by reducing it to an exclusively political dimension. I can only point out the naiveté of an approach that assumes all social events are within the control of human beings.

My own preference is for an eclectic and selective approach within the sociology of law. This means that I can benefit from the insights of Emile Durkheim in terms of his differentiation between repressive and restitutive law but ask why should they be mutually exclusive. It is not apparent why repressive laws should be less relevant in a community with an extensive division of labor. Nor, indeed, why a society that exhorts multiculturalism and tolerance for diversity of style, be it in clothing or sexual partners, will not also need to identify aspects of morality that can be considered shared between the polyglot social world in which appearance is no longer a guide to morality.

This approach does not assume a consensus. One of the ultimate ironies is that a social theorist such as Durkheim, whose underlying conceptual concern was the question, "How is social order possible?" should be dismissed by some as a naive consensus theorist.

I hope I am not enslaved by any one orientation. I am well aware that the Durkheimian perspective focuses on the consequences of punishment for morality and does not provide an understanding of the processes involved in the construction and reconstruction of what is presented as public morality. By describing it thus is not to decry its importance, but to recognize the limitations of this particular perspective. What is needed to overcome these limitations is an awareness of the intricacy, contradictions, and ambiguities of public morality and not to think we have captured it so readily as those theorists who paint with a broad brush think we can. This includes Marxists, Durkheimians, and cultural theorists.

In this study I have utilized many of the insights of the broad brush theorists but have added the refinements of the symbolic interactionists. If the interactionists are correct to insist that the understanding of social life requires an appreciation of the significance of symbolic representations and the potential meanings generated by the individual's involvement in group processes, then the focus group is the most appropriate tool of a research inquiry from an interactionist's perspective.

Policy questions can rarely be fully comprehended within the intellectual framework of any one social science discipline. Hence the need to be multidisciplinary and to allow the phenomena under study to dictate the course of the empirical analysis, rather than the theoretical limitations of any one social science paradigm.

This research was not started in order to develop theoretical ideas in sociology or criminology. My interest in sociological and criminological theory is based on the recognition that research is influenced by the assumptions we make about the subject of the inquiry. This is most apparent when we select the data for analysis, which is inevitably based on preconceived concepts, and that it is better to do this explicitly rather than implicitly.

Sensitivity to theoretical ideas is not the same as being dominated by them, however. The responsibility of writers about the cultural aspects of the human condition should be to remain faithful to the views of those they are describing and analyzing.

OUTLINE OF THE BOOK

The five chapters of this book relate to identifying and describing a credible and feasible form of intermediate punishment. This exercise in policy analysis required an excursion into theory and empirical inquiry. I have been engaged in research on penal policy in California since 1982. I have used a wide repertoire of empirical sources: interviews with policy makers, officials, wardens, correctional staff, and inmates; observational visits to prisons, courts, and the legislature; and a survey and a series of focus groups with criminal justice officials.

In chapter 1 I set out a case for a synthesis of denunciatory and retributive principles as the general justifying aim of the social institution of punishment. I have endeavored to spell out the significance of punishment for a community and how it relates to a citizen's fear of crime.

Both denunciatory and retributive approaches to sentencing require a range of proportional sentences related to the severity of the wrong to be punished. Where to start is referred to as the problem of "anchoring." An anchor is the wrong metaphor. What is most relevant for public credibility is not where it is anchored, inevitably out of sight below the surface, but what will "float" on the visible sea of public opinion.

Will intermediate sanctions float with the public? They will if the community has confidence in the rationale and operation of the criminal justice system. That confidence is more likely to be inspired by a penal philosophy that highlights community concerns, without rejecting the individual offender-oriented concerns of rehabilitation and individual deterrence. A denunciatory-retributive rationale provides a niche for intermediate sanctions—the middle of a range of sanctions—which reserves imprisonment for the most serious offenses, and probation and fines for the least serious.

In chapters 2 and 3 I outline the synchronic and diachronic factors that provided the context of the shifting penal debate: starting from the rehabilitative era and its subsequent decline in the 1960s, to the rediscovery of punishment through the back-to-justice movement. The current perceptions of penal debate are outlined, including the ubiquitous "penal crisis" so familiar to penological ears.

The 1990s will have to come to terms with two failed experiments that have left penology in a postmodernist confusion or penological limbo. These failures are associated with the efforts to solve the problem of crime by the advocates of rehabilitation over the past two hundred years, and by those who offered a quick fix in the 1980s with a promise to "get tough on crime." The direction of penal policy is still not certain, for we have yet to re-orient ourselves to these two failed experiments in social engineering. However, we are emerging from this era of penological limbo with a more balanced view of the multiple purposes of the criminal justice system and the priorities among these purposes.

The adjustment will have to balance the prison reductionists' concern about the apparent overuse of prisons with the public's anxiety about crime. Alongside the search for greater consistency and uniformity, demanded by the advocates of greater fairness and accountability in the system, is to be set the administrative concern for greater consistency and uniformity so as to achieve an effective, efficient, and coordinated criminal justice system.

In chapter 2 I discuss the philosophical context of the current debate about the direction of penal reform. Penal reform does not take place in a vacuum. Reforms are influenced by the ideological debates about the nature of crime and the purposes of punishment, as well as by the political and economic contexts that provide the opportunities and constraints on achieving reform. To understand the penal debate in the last decade of the twentieth century, I have outlined and discussed the recommendations of the California Blue Ribbon Commission Report, published in 1990, on the future of the penal system. This report was welcomed by many sections of the criminal justice world as an answer to the prayers of penal reformers and correctional administrators. But it would be well to heed Saint Teresa's warning that "more tears are shed over answered prayers than unanswered ones."

Chapters 4 and 5 focus on two aspects of implementing a policy of expanded intermediate sanctions: (1) the process of reform and (2) substantive policy considerations in the pursuit of a plausible intermediate sanction. In chapter 4 I discuss the importance of avoiding utopianism in the process of penal reform. One way is to improve the process of consultation and seek the opinions of those who will be responsible for its implementation. In chapter 5 I set out the findings from a consultative process using focus groups. Criminal justice officials from across California were invited to participate in discussions to identify aims, forms, and examples of intermediate sanctions.

The results of this empirical research in California lead me to suggest a form of intermediate sanction that can simultaneously provide for life-style intervention with offenders, satisfy retributive concerns about the targeted population of offenders, and provide for effective monitoring of offenders in community settings.

If intermediate sanctions are to be accepted by the public in California, officials believe that this form of penalty must require accountability from the offender, while providing the offender with a comprehensive range of services and enhanced methods of monitoring offender behavior in community settings. This will require a rethinking of the role of the probation service and an awareness that intermediate sanctions will be costly to operate. The questions will be whether they are more effective in controlling and changing offender behavior and whether they meet the citizens' concerns about crime in the community.

The premise of my argument has been the need to establish sanctions that have public and professional credibility. Thus I spell out the benefits and limitations of using focus groups as a means of assessing public and professional attitudes to penal reform.

PUNISHING CRIMINALS

PUN
CRI

1

Penal Aims and Public Confidence

The multiple objectives of the criminal justice system should be made clear and made public. The system is simultaneously about punishment and denunciation of the wrongful act, and the protection of the public through selective incapacitation and deterrence. It deals with humans who range from evil and dangerous to the pathetic and impoverished. The criminal justice system is a multipurpose system and has evolved over time to provide safeguards for citizens wrongly accused of crime, but it was never primarily intended as a social institution concerned with individualized welfare work. To a limited extent, it is possible to provide restitution to victims, rehabilitation for offenders, and crime prevention in the community, but only as secondary goals: goals more effectively pursued through the less stigmatizing institutions concerned with welfare, education, and social policies.

The limitations of the system should be made clear. The system is based on the need to respond, on the community's behalf, to violators of formal social rules embodied in the penal code. A failure to articulate the limitations of the criminal justice system will generate false expectations about the capabilities of the system. During a period of growth, the failure of the system to deliver what is promised is likely to result in a decline in public confidence.

A criminal justice system is by definition about social control. One of the first tasks of any society is to protect its citizens from antisocial behavior. A criminal justice system is inevitably linked to politics, but it is not reduced to politics as the definition of the antisocial takes shape. In a democracy the citizenry should play a crucial role in defining which acts are labeled as antisocial.

The criminal justice system is also about moral judgment, for the interpretation of antisocial becomes a matter of censuring those engaged in wrongful actions. Recognizing the control qualities of criminal justice does not deny the importance of the need to protect individuals by ensuring justice within the criminal process. As important is the need to encourage tolerance for the cultural practices of minorities, particularly in a society concerned with freedom and liberty. These concerns have become ever more important as western industrial societies have come to accept the multicultural nature of their societies. However, there needs to be a balance between individual and communal needs, and between cultural homogeneity and diversity. A society that fails to achieve this balance is not likely to provide a secure environment for its citizens.

The balance within the criminal justice system represented throughout the twentieth century as the "penal-welfare" system has not found popular support; the attempt to balance "punitive" and "constructive" measures has not been accepted by the public. Nor do I think the "constructive" approach is firmly established in the penal system in Britain (cf. Garland, 1989), other than in the professional ideology of probation officers and in the penal policy statements and rhetoric of influential pressure groups. In California it is difficult to find senior probation officers who still regard rehabilitation as their primary activity.

Currently, policy makers are debating the nature of community-based intermediate sanctions as an addition to the primary sanction of imprisonment. The introduction of "secondary punishment" to veer away from an over-reliance on the primary sanctions was

achieved in the past: capital punishment to transp
portation to imprisonment. This was achieved b
economically viable and an acceptable form of punis
as with the penitentiary, the rhetoric focused only o
to change individual offender behavior, additional elements were added to this "constructive" institution in the form of hard labor, to make it punitive.

What does this tell us? Punishment is not primarily a "constructive" institution in terms of its focus on an individual or individualized strategies to rehabilitate. The penitentiary as a place for transforming individuals into docile and acceptable citizens was a view shared by a range of religious and politically inspired reformers and commentators from John Howard to Michel Foucault. It is a view that was demonstrated to be wrong.

So what are the purposes of punishment? At the sentencing stage, they are "eclectic," as Nigel Walker points out with reference to the United Kingdom. Walker (1985) comments, "Nothing divides a committee like a discussion of the aims of punishment, as the ill-fated Royal Commission discovered in the nineteen-sixties." The Royal Commission on the Penal System in England and Wales was established in 1964. In 1966 it was dissolved, the only Royal Commission never to complete its report.

THE MULTIPLE OBJECTIVES OF THE PENAL SYSTEM

The U.S. Federal Sentencing Commission provides an example of the problem of establishing agreement on aims. After a year of "wrestling" with which rationale to adopt, it rejected Andrew Von Hirsch's exhortation to adopt a pure retributive model. It compromised and set forth four purposes of sentencing: (1) to reflect the seriousness of the offense, to promote respect for the law, and to provide just punishment for the offense; (2) to afford adequate deterrence to criminal conduct; (3) to protect the public from further crimes of the defendant; and (4) to provide the defendant with needed educational or vocational training, medical care, or other correctional treatment in the most effective manner.

Ilene Nagel's account of the discussions that led to the federal sentencing goals points to the policy makers unwillingness to "articulate a single purpose, such as just desert, nor to assign priorities to the four purposes ultimately delimited" (Nagel, 1990, p. 915). Nagel continues:

> As further evidence of its avoidance of theoretical orthodoxy, the Senate chose not to use the common term "just deserts"; substituted instead were the words "just punishment for the offense." No substantial leap of faith is required to interpret the congressional decision to substitute the words "punishment for the offense" for the words "deserts" as a showing that the statutory intent was to carve out a goal broader in meaning than the traditional just deserts emphasis on blameworthiness. (Nagel, 1990, p. 915)

Hence, crime control was being balanced with "just deserts" concerns so, "with multiple goals in mind, the judge was to consider the public's interest in preventing a recurrence of the offense as well as a just sentence for the convicted offender" (p. 916–917).

Missing from this formulation is any reference to the community and the values that define community. This omission is not made by the Canadian Law Reform Commission (1976), "We still need to do something about wrongful acts; to register our social disapproval, to publicly denounce them and to reaffirm the values violated by them."

In public statements and in academic analysis of penal policy and practice, there is a tendency to highlight the instrumental, the concrete, and the offender-oriented features of sentencing. For the practitioners, I assume, this is because it makes it more readily available as a justification of punishment to the lay public. The academics, on the other hand, are not usually affected by this consideration. The opposite might be more readily assumed. However, both assume a rationality of effectiveness that ignores the community-wide impact of punishment.

David Garland is critical of the Benthamite-Foucauldian academic tradition that sees punishment as exclusively concerned with society's instrumental control of the individual. The Foucauldian conception of punishment is described by Garland (1990) as "unduly instrumental and purposive, . . . given rise to an analytical framework which assumes in advance what one might term the control-oriented nature of modern punishment" (p. 1). This results in an "overstatement of punishment's positive political utility." Garland identifies an alternative Durkheimian interpretation of the significance of punishment.

> Foucault is insisting upon what one might call the Benthamite orientation of modern punishment. He is characterizing penal institutions, practices and discourses as so many instruments for the administration, direction and ordering of individual conduct. . . .
>
> So, although the modern state has a near-monopoly of the exercise of penal violence, a much wider population feels itself involved in the process of punishment, and supplies the context of social support and valorization within which state punishment takes place. Thus where Foucault sees only two parties involved in punishment—the controllers and the controlled—Durkheim insists upon a crucial third element, the onlookers, whose sentiments are first outraged and then reassured. (Garland, 1990, p. 5–8)

What is the impact of sentencing decisions on the onlookers as "receivers of law"? Deterrence theorists are concerned with the effectiveness of law in terms of its impact on the potential behavior of the lawbreaker. But denouncers are concerned with the impact on the values and beliefs of the public. Susan Silbey (1989) argues, "Instead of studying the effectiveness of law where it is actively intervening in people's lives, we should look to where it is least visible, where legal culture is being transmitted and learned in such ways that it quietly but routinely channels and shapes attitudes and behavior" (p. 24–25).

The pronouncements and decisions of those with a public profile in the criminal justice system affect the lives of ordinary citizens who are neither victims or defendants. Perhaps it is because of the concern with defendants and victims in the system that the media and politicians have found a ready audience among the general public for its stories about the inadequacies of the system. These stories exacerbate the fear of crime and encourage further anxieties associated with a breakdown of authority, which are translated into "law and order" concerns.

Perhaps the lack of regard for the public helps to explain the findings in the United Kingdom, cited by Walker and Mike Hough (1988). Respondents, asked about sentencing decisions made by the courts in Britain, regarded them as too lenient. But, when asked to match punishment to specific examples of crime, the respondents typically gave the same sentence as would have been imposed by the courts. These respondents underestimated the severity of penalties actually being given but assumed that the system is overly lenient. This might be a problem to be resolved through public education about sentencing practices, or it might be an indication of a suspicion by the public about the general orientation of a system as "out of balance" in terms of its goals.

In the United States, Nagel (1990) believes the public find many sentences handed out by the courts to be inappropriate: "year after year, public opinion polls confirmed the hiatus between sentences meted out by the court and the public's normative judgment of what should be appropriate sentences for given offense/offender patterns. On the whole, sentences served were considerably and consistently more lenient than public estimates of what ought to be the normative societal response" (p. 884).

Great care should be taken when interpreting the results of opinion polls, which can oversimplify the complexity of the issues involved and underestimate the ambiguities of responses. However, there can be little doubt about the unease felt by the U.S. public, and a crisis of expectations as to what the criminal justice system can deliver. In part this is an inevitable tension found in any criminal justice system in a democratic society, where the public demands protection, but within the constraints set by civil liberties and resources. It is a crisis of expectations also brought about by a multiplicity of goals and an ambiguity as to whose interest is being served by the system.

The criminal justice system should drop the pretense that it can rehabilitate and correct offender behavior as a matter of routine. That it can do so on a limited and less ambitious scale is a more realistic goal. Drop the notion that it is the offender, or even the victim, who is the client or customer of the system. Dispensing criminal justice is not a private matter between the courts, the professionals, the victims, and offenders. The customer, if that is the correct metaphor, is the public.

There are some, especially those who talk of a "swing of the pendulum," who see the terms *intermediate sanction* and *community corrections* as heralding a return to an era with a greater emphasis on rehabilitation. The Blue Ribbon Commission report refers to the need to change offender behavior, but it did not envisage a return to 1950s and 1960s style rehabilitation.

We know after two hundred years of experimenting with correctionalism that changing offender behavior is not easy. Correctionalism and rehabilitation were premised on the optimism of the Enlightenment and the promise of science. Criminologists in the nineteen century and early twentieth century thought that they had discovered the key to unlocking the mysteries of wrongful behavior, just as Darwin had discovered the theory of evolution.

The voyagers on the *Beagle*, however, were to undergo a relatively smooth passage compared with those who sought to understand the tides in the affairs of men—a journey that was to founder on the competing and complex mix of biological and social currents, a journey impeded by the shifting winds of culturally derived expectations and the existence, or not, of restraining norms, a journey undermined by the contingencies of choice and chance.

The complexities of the human interface with good and evil, deviance and conformity were never duplicated by the simple-minded, pain avoiding pleasure-seekers of utilitarian philosophy, nor by its offspring "Economic Man," nor by the medically inspired psychiatrists with their offers for cure, nor by the politically oriented conflict theorists, nor by the social determinists. They offer a view of mankind that does not exist. They are like "the maps which should be banned." As Gabriel, the hero in William Boyd's *Ice Cream Wars*, explained, because "they gave the world an order and reasonableness which it didn't possess."

But the influence of the social determinists can still be heard in criminological debate. The heyday of determinism was the period between the two world wars. A prominent sociologist, Harry Elmer Barnes, author of *The Story of Punishment,* wrote, "We must educate the public to accept the scientific view of the social-biological determination of conduct, which at once undermines the whole basis of the conventional theory of punishment and opens the way for the socio-medical treatment of the person who commits an anti-social act." Barnes wrote in 1930:

> Our crime system of criminal jurisprudence is wrong-headed and unscientific because, in the first place, it rests upon the fundamental assumption of the primary importance of detecting guilt and adjusting the punishment to the crime. Modern criminology insists on the contrary, that guilt with respect to a particular crime is often far from the most important point of issue. . . .
>
> Even more important, modern criminology entirely repudiates the objective of making the punishment fit the crime. In the first place, our modern knowledge of the nature of criminal conduct renders the whole conception of punishment as archaic. It is futile and foolish to punish a criminal as it is to punish a person suffering from a physical or mental disease. In the second place it is not the crime that needs to be dealt with but the criminal. (Barnes, 1930, p. 265)

The mode of thought described by Barnes as modern sought to eradicate the moral aspects of a community's response to crime.

The notion of modern employed by Barnes involves the compartmentalization of the world into fields of knowledge, derived from the deterministic socio-biological sciences under the control of the professional scientific elite—the brave new world of the specialists. Traditional responses to crime were characterized as archaic, wrong, unscientific because they looked backward at the guilty act of the offender, rather than forward toward the future conformity of the readjusted individual. Moral evaluation of the criminal act would be regarded by Barnes and the exponents of the modern as an irrelevant aspect of an outmoded way of life.

It would be as foolish to deny that human beings are influenced by biological and social influences as it is to assert that they are the product of them. But, in the context of western democratic societies, individuals expect rights and privileges as adult human beings. This type of society can only operate if those same individuals are held responsible for their behavior. In the postmodern world, expert opinion will have to sit alongside moral evaluation, rather than attempt to replace it. And while *choice* is an overused word in consumer-oriented capitalism, it is a key to describing the human condition. To paraphrase Marx, we make choices, but in circumstances not of our own choosing.

This view of criminal accountability does not overlook the injustices and inequalities of social conditions that result in the overrepresentation of poorer groups within the incarcerated population. However, the criminal justice system is not equipped to engage in the restructuring of society. It is not designed to redress the causes of crime, let alone social inequality. It cannot cope with resolving socially dysfunctional behavior, other than when it is manifested in breaches of the criminal law.

In the rest of this chapter, I elaborate on what the criminal justice system can realistically deliver in terms of serving the "other" receivers of sentencing policy (i.e., the community). To do this, it would help to clarify the issues if I distinguish between the four elements that constitute the intellectual framework of sentencing and penal practice.

- the general justifying aim or rationale of the social institutions of punishment
- the purposes of sentencing
- the principles determining the distribution of sentencing
- the goals of correctional institutions

The social institution of punishment is justified in the Blue Ribbon Commission's Report in California in terms of "protection of the public." A mix of sentencing purposes and principles is implied by this phrase, permitting a cocktail of the "punitive" elements of retribution, deterrence, incapacitation, and the "constructive" elements of rehabilitation and restitution.

A DENUNCIATORY-RETRIBUTIVE RATIONALE FOR PUNISHMENT

A denunciatory-retributive justification of the institutions of punishment with a rationale that gives priority to the community and its protection would be more likely to establish public confidence in the multiple purposes of punishment, including rehabilitation, at the sentencing and correctional stages. What is a denunciatory-retributive approach?

The rekindling of the "just deserts" approach has helped to restore the focus on the criminal act rather than the criminal actor. Rehabilitation, deterrence, and later incapacitation theory established a penological paradigm that focused primarily on the criminal actor. Retribution, through the re-emergence of the "justice" movement in the 1970s, refocused penological debate on the criminal act. Denunciation adds to this the rules that define these acts (i.e., the criminal law and the moral basis of these laws). A denunciatory-retributivist perspective encourages an examination of morality and its links with the rules embodied in the criminal code, rather than a focus on the criminal actor.

Retributive theorists do not provide a convincing explanation as to why we should punish. They present revenge as an end in itself.

They do not explain why there is a hierarchy of seriousness of crimes, only that there is one. The need to punish wrongdoing does not explain why we should nor what the consequences are if we do not do so. John Braithwaite and Philip Pettit (1990) maintain that "retributivism cannot provide a satisfactory set of answers to the key questions about sentencing and punishment; Why Punish? Who to Punish? and How to Punish? A synthesis of denunciation and retribution provides an answer. The denouncers offer an explanation of why we should punish, and the retributivists provide essential sentencing criteria, seeking to punish only the culpable with sanctions proportionate to the severity of the offense.

Retribution offers principles that should shape decisions at the sentencing stage about the distribution of punishment, rather than provide a general justifying rationale for the social institution of punishment. But it is a crucial aspect of sentencing that it, alone of all the theories, balances the need to demonstrate public disapproval through "deserved" punishment, against the need to protect the individual offender by limiting the extent of punishment through the principles of culpability and proportionality.

It was C. S. Lewis (1953) who offered this insight into the advantage of including in the aims of sentencing the retributivist concern with just desert. His criticism of rehabilitation is equally applicable to all "constructionist" and "consequentialist" approaches to punishment, including denunciation. He wrote, "The humanitarian theory removes from punishment the concept of desert. But the concept of desert is the only connecting link between punishment and justice. It is only as deserved or undeserved that a sentence can be just or unjust . . . we may very properly ask whether it is likely to deter others and to reform the criminal. But neither of these two last questions is a question about justice" (p. 225). Hence, it is crucial to include retributive principles in the aims of the criminal justice system because they set clear limits on that system as to who, how and when it can act against an individual. They provide the justification for civil rights within the criminal justice system.

Retributive principles provide a starting point for determining how much or what form of penalty is deserved. The principle of proportionality relates the seriousness of the penalty to the gravity of the offense to determine a condign form of punishment. The underlying principle of just deserts resolves into the practical question of "What will float with the sentencers and the public?" Obviously there are many technically illegalities that do not generate strong emotions and many routine offenses that are disposed of by cautions, discharges, and fines. Fines can be regarded as non-punitive penalties, and as such, "penalties are in effect licensing fees, different from other purchased permits in that price is often paid afterward rather than in advance" (Feinberg, 1965, p. 397).

Even so, the demarcation of different levels of antisocial behavior remains a moral evaluation. It is the denouncers' contention that sentencing is first and foremost a moral enterprise. Retribution brings our attention to the morality of the criminal act.

The practical sentencing decision of how to punish will be fashioned by a range of objectives that depends on the level of seriousness of the offense, considerations to do with resources, the sentencer's judgment about the most suitable disposition given the offense characteristics, and the offender's criminal profile. But it should also be influenced by reference to the community's disapproval and allow that disapproval to be expressed by the use of sanctions that have credibility in the community.

Until recently, the dominant penal paradigm sought to achieve the individual-instrumental penal goals of rehabilitation, incapacitation, and deterrence. The central focus of debate was on protecting the public by changing or controlling the behavior of the individual criminal. But what is the difference? If we control the criminal, we surely protect the public. To answer this, we need to understand the term *public*. Is it a mass of individuals, who in privatized bliss share only a concern with not being the victim of violence or fraud? The public is more than this. The idea of a public is founded on the idea of shared beliefs, which are institutionalized in social relations (i.e., a public cannot exist outside of a society).

Public protection is usually translated as meaning incapacitating the dangerous offenders and attempting to deter potential offenders from committing future crimes. It also can involve prevention and correctional efforts to change behavior of amenable offenders to prevent future law-breaking.

This prophylactic approach is readily approved of by policy makers concerned with "positive" public policy, which is reasonable and humane. But these do not capture the feeling of the public about many offenses. The community's anger is normally translated into the need to recognize the role of retribution in criminal justice policy. A mark of the success of the back-to-justice movement was to re-establish the notion of retribution in our formal policy documents.

But if we wish to speak seriously of punishment in the community, we must first understand the importance of punishment for the community and society. If we are more than a collection of individuals who share living space, we recognize that social relationships are vital. Society is made up of persistent configurations of relationships. These can be abstracted into core societal values that become enshrined in the criminal law and certainly cover more than just force and fraud (cf. Gottfredson and Hirschi) (e.g., matrimonial laws, blasphemy laws, religious observance laws, abortion, gambling, drinking and drug laws).

These values define what sort of society we are. They provide individuals with a set of established, taken-for-granted world views. They embody our essential moral views of right and wrong. As Emile Durkheim pointed out, those who breach laws are doing more than just the physical and financial damage they do to the individual victim, they are challenging the values of society, and as such they threaten the individual's definition of morality. Therefore, the purpose of punishment for the denouncer is not directed at the criminal act or the criminal actor, but at the values that define the rules embodied in the criminal law. The audience is neither the criminal nor victim but the public at large.

Could legal punishment, resulting in the deliberate infliction of human pain, be justified in terms of the moral condemnation of the criminal act? Theorists committed to the instrumental and offender oriented goals of deterrence, prevention, and reform, such as Herbert Hart, thought not. Primoratz replies, "By expressing condemnation of the misdeed committed, punishment vindicates the law broken, reaffirms the rights infringed, and demonstrates that the deed was an offence" (p. 151). In addition, denunciation reassures citizens that the values that underpin their way of life and the rights, rules and responsibilities that go with these values are worthy of condemnation if breached. They are symbolized as important because we are prepared to inflict harm on those who breach them. The importance of the retributive principles is that the act of denunciation should only involve those individuals who deserve to be punished. A limit to the denunciatory process is provided by the principle of deserts.

The impact of punishment is not a private matter between offender and victim, for it also involves the community's expectations about appropriate standards of behavior. It allows individuals living in the community to recognize that they share a common threat to their life-style and values that underpin that life-style. The criminal constitutes a threat to their civil liberties in terms of a threat to their property, physical well-being and shared values.

Cultural values provide the boundaries for understanding, describing and evaluating our social and natural world. These boundaries are prone to change, and their meanings cannot be automatically decoded. They depend on context and contrast. In complex, heterogeneous societies, the division of labor makes moral boundaries even more significant. Boundaries are necessarily comparative, as Anthony Cohen (1985) points out. Criminals can provide a focus and some degree of certainty in our otherwise fluctuating world. They fix our attention on the morality of the act, at a moment in time. This does not mean subsequently that the moral response to the criminal will not change in the future, nor that our definitions are detached from politics or conflict.

The criminal provides us with a living example of our moral boundaries; by our outrage we come to recognize our shared fears, rules of communal living and mutual interdependency. We collectively define what sort of people we are by denouncing the type of people we are not.

"WHAT WILL FLOAT?" PUBLIC CONFIDENCE IN SENTENCING POLICY

Punishment in the community is a key idea in the report of the California Blue Ribbon Commission published in 1990. The term *community*, although frequently used, is never defined. Its meaning is interpreted by its usage, which shows a limited conception of community as any location other than an institution, such as prison or a mental hospital. A more sociologically sensitive definition of community with a broader vision of community would help to provide insights into the nature of crime, and our awareness of the interrelationship between the community and the criminal justice system.

A broader vision of community would have a number of advantages and would have allowed for a greater exploitation of the interdependence between community and criminal justice policy.

1. It would bring with it an understanding of the need for greater liaison and consultation between the agencies within the criminal justice system and the public, to ensure that there is some correspondence in the way agencies and the public define and prioritize antisocial behavior (i.e., there is an issue of communication).
2. Crime has an impact on the economic assets and resources of the community both in terms of the direct economic effects of crime (e.g., closure of businesses through theft, the medical costs of victims of violent crimes) and indirectly by the way we respond to crime in terms of the expenditure on criminal justice agencies. As public funds are in use, we are entitled to ask whether the money is being used effectively and efficiently, both in terms of

goals and operational deployment (i.e., there is an issue of economics).

3. Questions of fairness and justice are not the exclusive property of the victim, offender or judge but can be asked from the broader perspective of justice in the community. This would encourage inputs to be made into policy debates from those who believe the system to be working against some sections of society in a way that is not intended by the criminal law (i.e., there is an issue of justice).
4. A community-wide perspective is more likely to challenge the professional and bureaucratic divisions within the criminal justice system that make it difficult to act in a coordinated and systematic fashion (i.e., there is an issue of effectiveness).
5. The search for the causes of crime, and the resolution of crime, requires an awareness of the role of the community as an influence on criminal behavior and the potential of utilizing the community as an aspect of criminal prevention policy (i.e., there is an issue of crime control).
6. A community approach will encourage the question, "Whose criminal justice system is it?" The community, as recipient of services from professional criminal justice agencies, is entitled to indicate the level of public confidence in those services (i.e., there is an issue of accountability and legitimacy).

The public's confusion about the effectiveness, fairness, cost, and priorities of the criminal justice system stems in part from attempts to address different audiences. We must decide whether the criminal justice system should primarily serve the community and its values, or the offenders, or the victims, or the professional participants in the system. Where do we start? With a theorist such as Foucault, or with the views of Californians in Fairfield, or

Londoners in Fulham, or with the subjective perceptions of convicted offenders?

In her article "When Probation Becomes More Dreaded Than Prison," Joan Petersilia argues that from the offender's perception, some forms of intermediate sanctions are more punitive than prison. This punitive view of intermediate sanctions should be developed to provide a punishment rationale for intermediate sanctions. But Petersilia's view will require a great public relations effort. This is no easy task, especially in the case of home confinement, which has been presented by one California official as "sitting around, watching TV, and getting someone pregnant" (Davies, 1990, p. 14).

But matching the severity of the penalty against the severity of the offense is not a matter of achieving balance based on the subjective impact on individual offenders or on the views of individual victims, or even the world view of eminent social theorists such as Foucault. It is a matter of public approval; the sentence must reassure the community that something has been done and that the punishment is appropriate.

Where do we "anchor" the range of appropriate punishments? This issue is vital for the retributive concern with proportionality: the seriousness of the offense must relate to the severity of the punishment. This cannot be done by some "cardinal" measure of absolutes but requires an "ordinal" approach. The problem is where to "anchor" the system (i.e., what gives the system some sense of stability or a point of comparative reference).

Hence the issue is "What will float?" not "Where is it anchored?" With sentencing policy there is no ocean floor on which to anchor the system of proportionality. Ocean floors are variable in depth as well as out of sight to the spectator, but at sea level that which floats is visible. And this is where the tariff of sentencing should start—with what is visible and floats on a sea of public acceptability.

From a denunciatory-retributive perspective, the system of proportionality should be floating on the waves of public consent, not hidden in the invisible mud of the ocean floor. The system of punishment must reserve its most serious form of acceptable punishment for the most serious case. It is a system that works down from top to bottom. In penological debate the public is always fascinated with the top end. For instance, capital punishment, while affecting relatively few offenders, has and does dominate debate about punishment.

Imprisonment can provide some degree of stability in the "floating" process because the public have confidence in it as an acceptable form of punishment. Thus the principle of interchangeability in punishment suggested by Morris and Tonry (1990) is undesirable. In their book *Between Prison and Probation* Morris and Tonry state, "It is the central question . . . . . to what extent can community-based punishments be combined with conditions of treatment to create punishments that both control and treat and are interchangeable with incarcerative sentences and with ordinary probation to create a comprehensive sentencing system?" (p. 180) An example of the principle of interchangeability of punishment is given by them, "we mentioned the state of Washington exchange rate of one day's community service for one day's confinement. . . . . We believe that non-incarcerative sentences can be devised that can meaningfully be said to be equivalent to imprisonment"(p. 100).

The danger of this principle of interchangeability is that by blurring the distinction between prison and non-prison sanctions, it could undermine public confidence in both. Convincing the public that punishment can exist without imprisonment is going to be difficult. If this latest attempt to provide an alternative to imprisonment is to have more success than previous attempts, much greater consideration should be given to the public's subjective fears and views about punishment in the community.

Morris and Tonry hold the view that for some criminals, prison is not particularly punitive. They point out "prisons provide a safe and more comfortable environment from which many of our street criminals come," and that, "punishments have different impacts on different people." True enough, but first, the equality of pain for equally culpable offenders is difficult to calibrate. Second, the offender's sensibilities are not the primary concern of a denunciatory-retributive perspective.

Morris and Tonry anticipate the criticism that the principle of interchangeability would undermine the principle of equality and proportionality in sentencing. They write, "First, from a moral perspective, the measure of punishment is not its objective appearance but its subjective impact. Our goal is to achieve a system of interchangeable punishment that the state and the offender would regard as comparable in their punitive effect on him. Second, we believe that non-incarcerative sentences can be devised that can meaningfully be said to be equivalent to imprisonment" (p. 93).

Of course, the measure of punishment must be in terms of its "subjective impact." But on whom? In a denunciatory-retributive model the subjective sensibilities that matter most are those of the public rather than those of the criminal, or even the victim. Furthermore, the blurring of that impact on the public is likely and undesirable, if it is maintained that intermediate sanctions, aimed at moderate level offenders, can in some way be equivalent to incarceration, which we reserve for the most serious offenders. This seems likely to undermine public confidence in all forms of sentences.

In an attempt to empirically test denunciatory theory, Nigel Walker and Catherine Marsh (1984) concluded that "for the great majority, a prison sentence stands for toughness," and that "a somewhat smaller majority regarded probation as 'mild'. . . and a symbol of leniency." In terms of Morris and Tonry's principle of interchangeability between incarcerative and non-incarcerative sentences, public perceptions of tough and soft sentencing options have to be kept in mind. A blurring of the tough-soft continuum runs the risk of undermining the one element of sentencing practice that has some degree of public confidence—incarceration.

Prison is one measure about which the public feel confident. Why is that? It is possible, if we adopt a perspective based on flow charts and statistics, to regard prisoners as the leftovers (i.e., the relatively small percentage of the numbers who enter the criminal justice system who end up in prison). Paul Embert and David

Kalinich wrote, "Prisoners in jails and prisons may be viewed as the 'leftovers'—those the criminal justice system has not 'filtered' out of prison into some other type of diversion or other correctional program" (p. 2). In a statistical sense, they are correct to refer to such prisoners as leftovers. But in the denunciatory-retributive approach, they are wrong, for prison is the relatively fixed aspect in terms of the public's imagination of the punitive elements of punishment.

Prisons have their critics, which include in England not only such penal reform groups as NACRO (National Association for the Care and Resettlement of Offenders) and the Howard League, but the Chief Inspector of Prisons in England and Wales, Judge Stephin Tumim. In February 1991, the 600-page Woolf Report, written by Lord Justice Woolf and Judge Tumim, was presented by the Home Office. This report dealt with the conditions that led to prison riots during April 1990 at Strangeways, Glen Parva, Dartmoor, Cardiff, Bristol, and Pucklechurch. Tumim speculated in the press, "Nobody is asking the basic question about why we are sending people to prison. It costs £20,000 a year to keep a man in jail and 58 percent go out and commit other offenses. . . . What we need is a new philosopher, a new Bentham, to work out what we are trying to achieve by sending people to prison in the first place" (*Independent*, February 25, 1991, p. 21).

The problem with this analysis is that it is imbued with Benthamite, utilitarian logic, which questions the utility of prison for the inmate and its potential deterrent or rehabilitative impact, but disregards another audience, the public. While the public's views on crime in Britain and the United States have been unnecessarily simplified when interpreted by opinion polls, the public have little problem in answering Judge Tumim's question in terms of the incapacitating role of prison for convicted criminals who constitute a danger to the public, as well as being a means of exacting just deserts on criminals and marking out the moral boundaries of our society.

There are penologists who regard prison as uncivilized (Vass, 1990), and indefensible in terms of penological rationale. Mathiesen

(1990) writes, "The theories of individual prevention—rehabilitation, incapacitation, individual defense—are unable to defend the prison. Neither is the other major theory of social defence—the theory of general prevention. And neither is, finally, the theory of justice. The prison does not have a defense, the prison is a fiasco in terms of its own purpose" (p. 137). British government penal policy-makers agree with Mathiesen on the use of deterrent arguments for prison. The British government policy document, published by the Home Office, "Crime, Justice and Protecting the Public" points out, "It is unrealistic to construct sentencing arrangements on the assumption [of the deterrence theorists] that most offenders will weigh up the possibilities in advance and base their conduct on rational calculations." But prison does enjoy public confidence as an acceptable form of punishment. This is recognized by Mathiesen, who refers to "a pervasive and persistent ideology of prison in our society" (p. 137). Despite its ineffectiveness in the terms he outlines above, the ideology of the prison persists, perhaps because it is one form of punishment that instills public confidence.

How do we assess public confidence? We could ask the public through a public opinion poll. In California, through the process of public initiatives, citizens are asked to participate in referenda each year. Thus, Californians enjoy greater voter participation on detailed aspects of public policy and give far more influence to those who vote than do most other systems of democracy, especially the parliamentary system found in Britain.

To what extend should penal policy be driven by public opinion? The system of retribution and denunciation needs to relate to public concerns with respect to what will float on the tide of shifting opinions. The criminal justice system should be more responsive to the public. The question of deserved punishment is not just a matter of technical or scientific resolution, but is an issue of moral judgment. In penal policy it should be understood that issues of passion and anger are at stake, and so they ought to be.

Recognizing the right of the public to express passion and anger does not mean that the administration of criminal justice should become a matter of unlicensed and faddish populism. Nor should it be shaped by the views of a single-minded pressure group. On the contrary, there should be a barrier to public participation in the details of sentencing policy. The state of California has allowed for considerable political intrusion into this process.

Why, having outlined a theory of punishment that demands input from community sources, do I now argue for restraint on that input?

First, an awareness that punishment can be affected by public passion and anger should make us sensitive to the need to proceed carefully because also in question is the fate of the individual who has been accused of a crime. The system is designed for revenge, but only under very carefully controlled circumstances. Ironically, it is retribution that ensures that a criminal justice system proceeds with due deliberation and through stages to establish clear indications of criminal culpability so as to protect the civil liberties of those brought into the system. Other theories, including those with liberal credentials such as rehabilitation, were happy to concede constitutional protection in pursuit of welfare intervention.

A second argument for imposing constraint on the influence of public opinion on sentencing policy is that democracy is a process of decision making that does not guarantee balanced or reasonable decisions, only majority ones. Some see the populace as unwitting dupes of political elites or of the community's own base instincts for revenge. In *The Justice Juggernaut* (1990), Ruth Gordon regards the growth of the American criminal justice system as a result of a neo-conservative law and order culture. Peter Waddington comments on her analysis. "According to Gordon, the politicians' exploitation of public fears and concerns has provided the motive power for the "justice juggernaut." In his review of *The Justice Juggernaut*, Waddington comments:

> The people, she implies, cannot be trusted to assess rationally the extent of the crime problem, identify its causes, and choose appropriate remedies. The American electorate has in her view, been manipulated by political elites and professional interest groups. The fact that she finds this a surprise is

> probably ample testimony to her naiveté. Democracy offers no promise that the decisions of politicians will be rational, nor that the minority rights will be safeguarded. The civilization of criminal justice policy has been achieved despite, not because of popular sentiment. (Waddington, 1991, p. 323)

Both writers express a jaundiced view of the nature of public sentiment and its impact on sentencing policy. Gordon sees political manipulation. But my research in California found criminal justice notables (judges, sheriffs, chief probation officers, public defenders, police chiefs, district attorneys) who believed that they could not sell the public whatever they liked; on the contrary, the typical reply to questions of reform was "Would the public buy it?"

Waddington is not alone in his concern about the impact of populist sentiment on criminal justice policy. However, it is unclear why it is deemed uncivilized for the public to express a demand to get tough on crime so as to protect themselves and the values that are seen as under threat by those who disregard the rules of a society.

Let me outline a third reason why public opinion alone should not be allowed to dictate sentencing policy. What does attitude and opinion poll sampling actually measure? Often no more than a superficial response to an unnecessarily polarized question, which can neither capture the sophistication of potential replies or the potential ambiguities that many respondents may feel, nor reflect the situational and context-bound nature of responses to the opinion questionnaire.

Public opinion can vary over time and between groups. The community is not a monolith. For this reason attitude measuring should be complemented by focus group analysis, which allows for more sophisticated responses. Mobilizing opinion around answers that allow only "yes" or "no" answers, or "for" or "against," will polarize and simplify many policy issues. In California, the introduction of mandatory prison sentencing laws for burglary, through the Public Initiative process, resulted in a sentencing policy that allows no discretion to deal with burglars of domestic premises, who might benefit from a non-custodial sentence.

Fourth, addressing the problem of public confidence in the criminal justice system is not a matter of more sensitive opinion polls to which the government responds. We should not make the mistake of assuming that public opinions and moral values are synonymous. David Piachaud (1991) makes the point that social policy in Britain in the 1980s was lacking in values and principles, "leaving, as it sometimes seems, cultural and social values to be prescribed by the editor of the *Sun* [newspaper, London]" (p. 223). He does not see this as the only alternative, and he calls for "higher expectations of citizens and greater demands made of citizens if we are to live in a truly civilized society" (p. 224). He writes:

> No democratic government can, or should attempt to impose a set of uniform political beliefs. Yet there are certain values about which there is a very broad consensus. There would be a wide ranging support for the assertion and promotion by government of humane, liberal, tolerant, social values that give equal respect to all, of a work ethic which stresses the responsibility of all those who can work for society, of rights to good health care and education as well as rights to life and liberty, of the importance of non-violence in society and respect for others. (p. 223)

A fifth reason why we should recognize the need to start with public opinion but not stop there relates to knowledge and experience of the criminal justice system. Opinions and passions are the starting point of the process of punishment; they are not its ends. How best to achieve protection of the public requires expertise and knowledge. Judgments have to be made about the resource implications of sentencing policy. Policy makers need to have an understanding of the technical and administrative complexities that constitute the criminal justice system, as well as a knowledge of criminal law and its constitutional implications.

Popular opinion and public sentiments provide the beginning but not the end of a denunciatory-retributive approach to sentencing in democratic societies. The five arguments outlined above recognize some of the pitfalls of populism. But public opinions and sentiments cannot be ignored if public confidence is to be maintained in the criminal justice system.

Nor does the adoption of a denunciatory-retributivist perspective lead to the inference that the system must necessarily become more punitive. First, the principles of distribution of punishment derived from a retributive logic require penalties to be appropriate or deserved, not simply punitive, regardless of culpability or the level of severity of the offense. The task is to find a level of sanctions that will "float" with respect to public opinion. Second, in interpreting public opinion we should not fall into the assumption that what is wanted is tougher sentences.

Surveys of public attitudes have found that the public is not exclusively punitively oriented. Gottfredson, Warner, and Taylor (1988) report in their U.S. study, "Contrary to general belief, we found the general public not to be especially punitive—rather they stress more utilitarian goals, such as rehabilitation, deterrence and incapacitation" (p. 45). Public opinion is more complex and there is sufficient evidence from surveys and focus group inquiries in Britain and the United States that the public are aware of the need to balance the competing goals and complex issues when sentencing offenders, and are not exclusively punitive in outlook. Once there is confidence in a system, then the diverse aims of sentencing can be understood and supported by the public.

2

Penal Limbo: Answered Prayers?

As we approach the twenty-first century, penal goals have become more prosaic. We are more cautious about attributing grand objectives to our penal machinery and institutions. In the United States a more honest description of the impact of incarceration would require a new word to replace the term *corrections*. By the end of the twentieth century the ambitious mission statement associated with previous penal epochs is missing from policy documents.

One reason for this has to do with two failed experiments in penal intervention. One started in the last decade of the eighteenth century with the introduction of the penitentiary, with its promise to change men's souls, minds, and behavior. This first experiment in rehabilitation was committed to the proposition that human behavior is malleable. Originally, change in criminal life-styles was promised as a result of religious intervention. However, during the nineteenth and twentieth centuries, religion was replaced by the new orthodoxy offered by scientific experts in human analysis and social engineering.

One consequence of a penal paradigm based on the scientific insights of these professional experts was the separation of morality from the response to crime. The defusing of the moral aspects of sentencing was at the same time the major achievement of the socio-psychological paradigm and its greatest weakness. The detachment of the professional replaced the anger of the community as the acceptable face of crime control in the social welfare societies of the twentieth century.

The second experiment barely lasted a decade. On both sides of the Atlantic the 1980s saw a policy of penal expansion, with a massive prison-building program as the flagship of a law and order approach that believed that if it could incarcerate sufficient offenders, steadily rising crime rates could be stemmed. Governments were unable to build prisons at a rate faster than the courts were able to fill them. Hence, despite the massive building programs, the prisons in California remained overcrowded. By the end of the 1980s the high costs of this approach and the failure to dent the rising crime figures lent some urgency to the search for sentences that were less costly than imprisonment.

By the end of the twentieth century we are still in the penal limbo caused by the disillusionment brought about by the unfulfilled, if different, promises made by the exponents of rehabilitation and the "get tough on crime" approach. Both the socio-psychological experts and the politicians were unable to deliver the goods. Crime was not so easily tackled as the enthusiasts for rehabilitation or the prison expansionists had promised.

The publication in 1990 of the Blue Ribbon Commission Report in California rekindled the fires of those who had retained an ideological commitment to the cause of rehabilitating offenders. After two hundred years of the idea that to change offenders it was best to remove them from the community and its crimogenic influences, came the official acceptance of the view that prisons make offenders less likely to lead law-abiding lives after release. By the 1990s the ideological reductionists who advocated less reliance on prisons for rehabilitative or humanitarian grounds were joined by the pragmatic reductionists who recognized that the criminal justice system did not have the infrastructure or the resources to maintain the expansion that occurred during the 1980s.

THE RISE, DEMISE, AND REDEFINITION OF REHABILITATION

We know after two hundred years of experimenting with correctionalism that changing offender behavior is not easy. Correctionalism and rehabilitation and the belief in the power of prisons to change offenders' behavior were premised on the optimism of the Enlightenment and the promise of science. The introduction of penitentiaries in the last decade of the eighteenth century did secure a hold as the dominant penological paradigm until a century later.

The Californian penal system was famous, and in later years notorious, for its commitment to the idea of reformation of the offender, a commitment powerfully illustrated by faith in the indeterminate system of sentencing, introduced in 1917. The following year, the California Supreme Court stated in support of these reforms:

> It is generally recognized by the courts and by modern penologists that the purpose of the indeterminate sentencing law is to mitigate the punishment which would otherwise be imposed upon the offender. These laws place emphasis upon the reformation of the offender. They seek to make the punishment fit the criminal rather than the crime. They endeavor to put before the prisoner great incentive to well-doing in order that his will to do well should be strengthened and confirmed by the habit of well-doing. (California Supreme Court, 1918)

In 1944 the Californian system became wholly indeterminate. The sentence laid down by law for common felonies referred only to a minimum and maximum term (e.g., one year to fifteen). On conviction, the sentencing judge would indicate that the length was for the "term prescribed by law." Criminals were viewed as suffering from a social or personality disorder that could be diagnosed and prescribed, in the same style as a medical cure. The heyday of the modernist age and the last stage of the Enlightenment formulated a logic of intervention with criminals whereby the scientific insights of medicine, psychiatry, nutritionists, environmental reformers, educational specialists, and social reformers would solve the problems of crime along with those of poverty and inequality. The promise was to do this in the technical, moral free world of professional specialists.

Moral responses to criminal acts were now outdated. The scientific professionals were the new priests, dispensing knowledge, not morality. This penal orthodoxy was commonplace in the Western world until the 1960s. It was an orthodoxy based on the assumption that human behavior could be reprogrammed in a systematic and purposeful way to produce correct behavior. It was a matter of expertise rather than morality.

The contention that rehabilitation could provide a marked decrease in the number of recidivists did not withstand empirical examination. We were too slow to learn the lesson that regardless of the name of the institution, or the motives of those who run them, prisons are not places likely to reform offenders. By the 1960s the lack of empirically observable success led to the gloomy prognosis that nothing worked. During the 1960s the coalition of interests that made up the rehabilitative lobby in Europe and North America began to fall apart. A lack of observable success was one reason; another was the underlying assumptions that made up this remarkable penal movement.

Rehabilitation was made up of a number of constituent interests: (1) the science-based professionals who through medicine, nutrition or psychiatry would diagnose and cure criminal behavior; (2) those who believed in the power of work and who put their faith in the impact of training and acquiring the discipline of work; (3) those who approached the criminal as in need of help through case work and welfare assistance; (4) those who believed in the power of moral awakening, either through religion or more recently via confronting offenders with the harm they have done; (5) those who simply believed in the need to treat inmates in a more humane way by removing the degrading and brutalizing aspects of prison life;

and (6) the social engineers who identified poverty as the root of all social problems and who put their faith in growing affluence and the welfare state—a faith dashed on the rocks of an unprecedented rise in recorded crime that was matched only by the growing postwar affluence of the 1950s. In Britain, the authors of the Home Office report "Penal Practice in a Changing Society" lamented, "It is a disquieting feature of our society that in the years since the end of the war, rising standards in material prosperity, education and social welfare have brought no decrease in the high rate of crime reached during the war; on the contrary, crime has increased and is still increasing" (p. 1).

The consensus was shattered by the realization in the 1960s that not everyone shared the view that crime was wrong. The politicization of penal, welfare and social policy led radicals to conclude that crime was simply a matter of political repression and struggle. One's stance depended on one's perspectives.

Another nail in the disintegrating coffin of rehabilitation was the realization that if the aim was to change the future behavior of offenders, then by the 1960s there existed a technology of surgery and drug treatment that could do just that. The liberal reformers and the civil rights component of the coalition started to balk at the efficacy of drug implants and surgical techniques to produce docile inmates and citizens. When medical intervention took these more dramatic forms, many of the liberal reformers, who identified rehabilitation as more humane, came to realize that punishment might be a better alternative. Hence, the liberal element of the 1970s constituency to support the back-to-justice movement.

The back-to-justice approach also derived considerable momentum from the disillusionment about the operation of the individualized system of sentencing. Critics pointed out the sentencing disparities for those convicted of similar offenses and the potential and actual abuses of the system of discretionary justice now carried out far away from the public scrutiny. More honesty, openness and certainty in punishment were qualities that reformers demanded from all political perspectives.

In California, the justice approach provided the penological rationale for the Uniform and Determinate Sentencing Law of 1976. By the early 1980s it became apparent that the reformed sentencing system was not working with a logic consistent with a justice approach. It was driven more by a concern with appearing to be tough on crime than with consistency and proportionality. Sentencing reforms were ad hoc. Parts of the criminal justice system were heading in different directions at the same time, far beyond the usual eclectism found in any punishment system in a complex society. One obvious example of this was the continuous and politically inspired tinkering with sentence lengths by the legislature and the introduction of mandatory sentences that took no account of resource consequences. The result was a doubling of the state's prison population in a decade and prison overcrowding.

A combination of liberal and pragmatic reductionists won the argument in California; the Blue Ribbon Commission Report is even explicitly reductionist. Within the context of a rapidly growing penal population, the commission concluded that it is in the state's interest, "to fund, regulate and monitor the expansion of these additional intermediate options in an effort to reduce the rate of increase of state prison and jail population without compromising public safety" (p. 4).

THE BLUE RIBBON COMMISSION'S REPORT IN CALIFORNIA

The Blue Ribbon Commission on Inmate Population Management was given statutory authority by Senator Robert Presley's Senate Bill 279 and introduced into the California legislature in 1987. The commission started work in the summer of 1988 and presented its report to the governor and the legislature on January 29, 1990. Despite the narrowness of the title, which was chosen to focus upon the management of the incarcerated, the commission provided a broad vision of an entire criminal justice system that in a decade had experienced rapid and unplanned expansion.

In presenting the commission's report, its chair, Grover Trask II, the district attorney from Riverside County wrote in the preface to the report, "The Commission has come to the predominant conclusion that the criminal justice system in California is out of balance. Additional punishment options must be expanded to reduce overcrowding while protecting public safety."

The report provided a comprehensive picture of a criminal justice system under considerable pressure from the number of defendants passing through it. The report's most significant contribution to the development of penal policy was its recommendation to expand the use of community-based intermediate sanctions for both sentenced offenders and parolees who infringed their parole conditions.

The success of the report lay in its ability to reconcile three different criminal justice constituencies. The recommendations were able to accommodate the more liberal commissioners, those most concerned with prevention and rehabilitation, appointed to the commission by the Democratic dominated legislature; the conservatives concerned more with punishment and surveillance, appointed by the Republican Governor George Deukmejian; and the professionals and administrators on the commission who were concerned with the pragmatic issues of how to cope with a system that was being swamped by numbers.

Despite its title, the report does not provide any recommendations on how to manage inmate populations in overcrowded institutions from the perspective of those who run prisons. The report's comprehensive and broad interpretation of its brief was in itself a surprise. The governor in signing the bill to establish the commission made the following points in his letter to the Senate in Sacramento:

> The primary reasons for prison overcrowding are that excessive numbers of criminals are violating the laws that we have enacted and because there is a lack of sufficient capacity in our state prison and local jail systems. The best way to address this issue is to continue to remove convicted felons from

> neighborhoods and to continue the aggressive prison expansion program which we are jointly supporting.
>
> It would be disappointing if this commission views its task as merely suggesting ways in which to put fewer criminals in prison or to shorten their terms. We should never forget that when only a small percentage of felons were sent to prison, the public expressed its strong concern.
>
> The commission can perform a positive service if it suggests methods by which incarceration would be achieved more economically, or recommends alternative methods which would absolutely insure that public safety is protected. The present pilot program on home electronic surveillance may hold out some hope for more economical methodology.
>
> Finally, while the cost of maintaining our prison system must be of concern, the vastly more important concern must be the protection of public safety. The right of our families and children to be secure from the threat of violent crime is a paramount concern of my administration and cannot be compromised simply in the name of economy. (Deukmejian, 1987, p. 1)

However, the 132-page report tackles the problems of correctional overcrowding not just as an issue to be resolved by prisons at back end of the system, but as an issue requiring a comprehensive and systematic re-evaluation of the entire state and local criminal justice system—from prevention through discharge of jurisdiction.

The Blue Ribbon Commission did not provide a blueprint for the California criminal justice system of the twenty-first century. Instead, it comprehensively described the problems of a system that had expanded with unprecedented speed, without the benefit of a systematic evaluation of its efforts, other than to placate the desire "to get tough on crime."

A report of this size and scope was bound to stimulate discussion to interpret and clarify its conclusions and thirty-eight recommendations. The commission's description of the system as "out of balance" did not imply that this was another swing of the pendulum away from tough to softer approaches to crime—a pendulum swinging on an already imbalanced system is likely to cause disaster. Despite some of the language in the report and the views of some of the commissioners, the report in general suggests that a correctional system can be multipurposed. It did not say that the jail and prison building program should stop. It recommended, however, that we look at corrections as a part of the criminal justice system as a whole.

The Blue Ribbon Commission described a penal system that had undergone a dramatic change in size (Table 2.1). The prison population quadrupled over the decade from 22,500 in 1979 to 86,000 in 1989; new construction between 1982 and 1990 resulted in an additional 40,000 prison beds and 25,500 jail beds. Construction continues. A five-year projection estimates that the daily average population of incarcerated offenders will be a quarter of a million by 1994.

But despite the growth, the Blue Ribbon Commission concluded "By the time the current expansion program is constructed in 1994, the projected population will be more overcrowded than it is today."

Table 2.1
Inmate Population Projections—California

	1989	1994	Percentage Increase
California Department of Corrections	86,746	136,640	58
California Youth Authority	8,329	9,478	14
County jails	67,956	93,003	37
Juvenile facilities	8,999	10,142	13
TOTAL	172,030	249,203	45%

(*Source*: Blue Ribbon Commission, p. 3)

The commission identified a number of problems facing the criminal justice system, the first and most obvious being overcrowding in penal institutions. Overcrowding results in the early release of sentenced offenders because of litigation about conditions that do not meet the legal standards for housing inmates. It adds to security and safety problems for staff and inmates. It concentrates the mind of administrators on the mundane operational tasks of transportation, feeding, and bedding, and leaves little money, energy, or space for programs to help those inmates who might choose to re-evaluate and redirect their lives.

We cannot expect the prison population to decline in the near future. On the contrary, prison populations are likely to increase as the "war on drugs" begun in the late 1980s continues to result in more arrests and incarcerations. The Blue Ribbon Commission found that

- adult felony drug arrests in 1988 (258,510) surpassed arrests for property offenders (152,992) during that same period. (p. 24)
- test results from April through June 1988 showed an increase of positive results [these tests exclude marijuana and alcohol], rising to 73 percent of Los Angeles arrestees and 77 percent of San Diego arrestees. (p. 68)
- drug charges were a known factor in 56 percent of all parole revocation actions. (p. 71)

The second problem identified by the Blue Ribbon Commission concerns the financial consequences of prison expansion. The prison construction cost brings with it the future liability for the operating costs of prisons. The prison construction program will have cost $3.2 billion by 1994. By this date, the annual operational costs for the Department of Corrections will be $4 billion, which is $1 billion more than the entire local and state corrections system cost in 1989. State budget negotiations will not be made any easier by this legacy of the 1980s.

A third problem involves public safety. The California correctional system is characterized as the most expensive and biggest set of revolving doors in the world, by Brian Taugher, who represented the California attorney general on the commission. The report found a high turnover of offenders and parole violators who stayed for relatively short periods of time in the state prisons. Half of the inmates admitted to state prisons in 1989 were released in less than a year. In 1988, there were 5,000 non-parolees who served three months or less in state prison and 8,000 who served six months or less.

A significant proportion of inmates has frequent, if relatively short, periods of time in state prison, a phenomenon summed up by Messinger and Berocochea (1990) as, "Don't Stay Too Long But Do Come Back Soon." Typically these short-term inmates build up a significant tally of time in custody on the "installment plan." On average they spend 7.9 months on pretrial and presentenced jail hold; then with half remission in state prison through the Work Incentive Scheme, they are released to return within six months on parole violations.

Half of admissions to state prison in 1989 were parolees. The report found that in 1988, of the parole violators returned to the Department of Corrections, 15,000 served three months or less and 23,000 served six months or less. of those paroled in the first six months of 1987, 67 percent were returned to prison. The parole violators rate rose from 15 percent in 1977 to 70 percent by 1989. The Department of Corrections's projection for parole violators returned to prison in 1994 is 83,000.

This data from the Blue Ribbon Commission on the short-term inmate leads to the conclusion that the state prisons are holding a population that would have been in county jails ten years ago. Many of those who served six months or less have drug problems, and their subsequent parole violator status indicates that they are unlikely to move away from crime-prone life-styles after release.

Prisons are costly institutions. For 1990 the average cost per inmate is $19,000 a year in state prison. The question raised by the Blue Ribbon Commission is this: Are we making the most effective use of the money spent on offenders? The Blue Ribbon Commission's report did not think so in that the incapacitative effect of imprisonment with this population is reduced to a few months; that a prison sentence seems to have very little deterrent impact on this population; that there are few rehabilitative programs in prisons; that offenders are bounced around between different agencies in their short but persistent involvement with the system; and that there is little continuous authority and surveillance to control and monitor their behavior.

They concluded, "It is questionable as to whether long-term public safety is being served or enhanced by certain non-violent new commitments or parole violators going to state prison for less than one year" (p. 41).

The commission identified a fourfold approach to solving the problems it described in its report. The commission's recommended solution to the prison and jail overcrowding problem is through an approach involving:

- changes in sentencing practices
- adoption of a Community Corrections Act
- changes in corrections practices such as parole revocation procedures
- additional construction of prisons, jails, youth facilities and community corrections facilities as necessary (Blue Ribbon Commission, p. 123)

Of the thirty-eight recommendations in the Blue Ribbon Commission's report, the most far-reaching concerned the expansion of punishment options. In effect, this became a discussion on the possible form, role and acceptability of intermediate sanctions and the adoption of a Community Corrections Act. They described the potential advantages of expanding the use of intermediate sanctions:

> These sanctions would provide a continuum of choices for judges and parole authorities, as well as provide options

> which are both substantially more restrictive and structured than present-day routine probation. They would also provide several choices that include close surveillance in community settings. The commission has concluded that these sanctions would not compromise public safety if used with discretion with the appropriate offender population. In fact, the commission believes that these sanctions will enhance public safety over the long term with reduced recidivism. (Blue Ribbon Commission, p. 49)

Greater use of intermediate sanctions was to be encouraged through the adoption of a Community Corrections Act, which would create "a partnership" between state and local government to significantly expand intermediate community sanctions for offenders. The goal of the act should be:

> To enhance public safety by encouraging the development and implementation of highly structured intermediate community sanction between traditional probation and incarceration. Such sanctions should function as punishment, as well as provide the offender with the opportunity through programs, training and work to change their criminal behavior. (Blue Ribbon Commission, p. 114)

In broad terms, a greater use of intermediate sanctions would suggest three practical strategies: (1) backing down the system to keep less serious offenders out of secure facilities; (2) making more programs available to those in custody and for working with offenders in community settings; (3) establishing new community correctional centers.

In the report the commissioners identified the potential target population for community corrections as those offenders going to state prison for less than one year, with an emphasis on those sent for six months or less, and parolees returned to state prison for six months or less. For those under the jurisdiction of the California Youth Authority, they see community corrections as being targeted at the less serious non-violent offenders from the juvenile court, parole violators, and offenders in the last 120 days of their sentence. In the counties they see community corrections as valid for those given jail sentences and for some on pre-sentence detention. They stress that this target population, "should be further limited to non-violent property offenders including drug abusers. Emphasis should be on first-time offenders and those without a significant criminal career" (p. 115).

Whatever the penological soundness of the arguments described in the Blue Ribbon Commission's report, political and economic factors are bound to shape the reception and evaluation of the ideas promoted. It is more realistic to regard this report as a description of a state of affairs and an agenda of future policy discussions than a prospective blueprint.

In 1990 a focus group study was used to test the response of criminal justice officials to the ideas in the Blue Ribbon Commission report (Davies, 1990). For the majority of panelists in the focus groups, the commission did a great service to the criminal justice system by spelling out the complexities and problems the system faced in California. The description of the system and its problems was consistent with the realities as the majority of panelists saw them.

A few congratulated the commissioners and expressed the hope that there would be a follow-up to the report to ensure some future changes in penal policy. One judge criticized the report as a waste of money for everyone already knew the problems described by the commission. But most concurred with the following view: "It has given us an opportunity to explore different options. It's making us think and rethink the system which is not working now, and I think that was the purpose of the Blue Ribbon panel." (Davies, 1990, p. 3)

Several panelists disagreed with some of the assumptions and conclusions of the report. Four district attorneys—"my middle name is Thomas"—doubted the conclusion about the inefficacy of imprisonment for short-term inmates. However, prosecutors seeking convictions for felonies, as one judge explained, are unlikely to see the use of prison even for short terms as a problem, "as the one thing the district attorney is usually concerned about is getting another 'prison prior' on the person" (Davies, 1990, p. 3). One district attorney offered the view that the worst of the drug crisis was over, and hence the likelihood of future overcrowding would be reduced.

The swing of the pendulum back toward an era of rehabilitation after a decade of getting tough on crime was an interpretation of the report that worried some but was approved by others. The majority, which included those district attorneys who were critical of some of the assumptions made in the report, saw no problem with intermediate sanctions in principle. They are routinely in use at present. The problem of expanding their use would come first from how to finance the expansion and second in determining the target population.

There was only one panelist, a chief of police, who maintained that the report was based on wrong assumptions and reached incorrect conclusions. He interpreted the report as an about-face, whereas what is needed, in his eyes, is more of the same. He challenged the prison population projection figures:

> I think those projections are just as clearly wrong as they possibly can be. They are based upon a state that did not do anything for several years. All through the 1960s and the 1970s, we did very little. We were letting them out of jails. We had probation subsidy, all these phoney systems to deal with the criminal element. Now we have finally got tough in the 1980s and start putting them in prison.
>
> The criminal element out there is not infinite. It's finite. This view that it is going to go on forever (rising numbers in prisons) through the 1990s and into the next century with billions and billions of dollars spent, I don't believe that. I think there is a point where it is going to start levelling off. We are going to have to find that point.
>
> I read this report and what it says is that the criminals have us just exactly where they want us. We are on the run again.

> We are going to back away from the approach that has been working.
>
> I can show you now where it is starting to level off in my city, substantially levelling off in my city, even though the population is increasing, even though some of the social problems have increased and gotten worse.
>
> What I am saying is that our tough policy has begun to pay off. Now we want to back away from that because we are going to spend too much money. I look in here and it says we are spending 6 percent on corrections. That is the first order of business for government to make sure people are safe. (Davies, 1990, p. 3–4)

From the same county came a more typical endorsement in support of the thrust of change suggested by the Blue Ribbon Commission:

> I have to believe that the thrust of things in the Blue Ribbon Commission is the wave of the future. I believe we will see support for legislation. I believe we have the opportunity, if we work together and understand what we are trying to do, to provide something we are not now providing, truth, sanctions and an opportunity for rehabilitation. We could do it through the use of intermediate sanctions. (Davies, 1990, p. 4)

The Blue Ribbon Commission argued that public protection would be greater if there were more opportunities for rehabilitation. The authors of the Blue Ribbon Commission report think this is more likely, "if offenders are kept in the community"; then "offenders retain their ties to family, jobs, and the community, thereby ultimately enhancing the likelihood of a successful reintegration into the community." Ironically, many panelists felt that the community was the source of criminality, and a list of community-based causes of crime was identified, which included a lack of jobs, peer pressure, drug subculture, family and housing problems.

While most panelists approved of the expansion of intermediate sanctions if funds were available locally, they balked at the idea of money from state sources. A panelist commented, "something which needs to be overcome is the county's suspicion that a partnership with the state is like tying your leg to an anchor and throwing it overboard" (Davies, 1991, p. 5).

The Blue Ribbon Commission had recommended that money made available to the counties from state agencies like the California Department of Corrections (CDC) to build shared jail facilities, which should ease both state and local overcrowding, while making programs available to inmates. This approach is based on the assumption, in 1990, that state agencies, especially the CDC, have a relatively more stable source of funding. Hence, they saw this as a way of getting money to the counties. By 1992 the availability of funding from state sources was looking less likely as the extent of the state budget deficit was recognized. But county officials were not tempted by the offer of money if it involved a partnership with state agencies.

The counties' concern over financing took two forms: (1) that funding subsidies might start off high but would be reduced in subsequent years, or not increased in line with inflationary costs; (2) that the state would mandate unacceptable conditions, which would erode any financial gains made by the counties, through state-imposed conditions and standards on institutional programs.

One attempt to overcome these anxieties was found in Senate Bill 2000 in California in 1990. This bill, introduced by Senator Presley, provided for Community Correctional Centers for drug abusers. The bill made the agreement between state and county a matter of voluntary, long-term contractual negotiations. It guaranteed 50 percent of bed space to the counties. The state agency would pay all of the construction costs of the facility; the operational costs would be shared equally between the state and the county. Despite this, county officials were skeptical of the long-term financial viability of such an arrangement.

The report of the Blue Ribbon Commission showed that the hunt was on for a secondary sanction that would not replace imprisonment but would provide a step in the hierarchy of penalties available to the courts, a sanction that would function as an intermediate punishment. The report targeted prison-bound inmate populations, focusing on property offenders, and effectively highlighted the issue of what to do with persistent thieves and burglars if we do not send them to prison. The report stressed the need for alternatives that could be regarded as punishment, while recognizing the failure of imprisonment in deterrent and rehabilitative terms.

Although the report retained a commitment to the goal of rehabilitation, it does not reply on an exclusively rehabilitative rationale. Rehabilitation is in part served by not using incarceration. The authors referred to a rehabilitative approach based on accountability and confronting offenders with their crimes.

The reductionist logic of the Blue Ribbon Commission's report was evident: "Paramount emphasis should be placed on those areas that will significantly lessen the numerical impact on prison and jail populations" (p. 123). The report focused on sentencing policy and the need to extend the range of penalties so as to have a continuum of penalties, based on combinations of existing community sanctions. Hence, the search for intermediate penalties.

Imprisonment is not the only form of punishment, according to the report. The loss of liberty is the common currency of punishment, which can be achieved by degrees of supervision and surveillance that do not require incarceration for all but the most serious of crimes. While stressing that it does not envisage a "move toward a wholesale relaxation of incarceration as a punishment option," the commission suggests: "There are increasing indications that adequate control and supervision outside of confinement is not only possible but can be more cost-effective and purposeful for certain offenders. Highly structured programming incorporates both accountability and possibilities of behavioral change for the offender" (Blue Ribbon Commission, p. 48).

Protection of the public is recognized as the primary responsibility of the criminal justice system, and the Blue Ribbon Report makes no secret of the need for a punitive element in sentencing. But the report reflects the realization that there is no one simple goal for a criminal justice system. Crime prevention, for instance, is spelled out in the report.

The Blue Ribbon Commission authors distinguish between primary, secondary, and tertiary prevention. Primary prevention aims at a young target population and stresses the importance of social and economic factors and the general welfare of the population in preventing crime:

> Good education, health care, shelter, nutrition, recreation, and employment opportunities represent forms of primary prevention. Unemployment and the lack of formal education are significant contributing factors to the level of criminal conduct in contemporary society. A well-educated and working population are much less likely to be involved in crimes such as robbery, the trafficking of narcotics and other illegal drugs, and certain property crimes such as burglary. (Blue Ribbon Commission, p. 12)

Secondary prevention targets individuals who are at risk and have been identified by criminal, welfare, or educational agencies as likely to require intervention to prevent a drift toward crime.

Tertiary prevention deals with those who have been found guilty of committing an offense and involves efforts to rehabilitate them. Clearly, intermediate sanctions are an aspect of tertiary prevention for they attempt to promote a more law-abiding life-style.

Despite very few references to rehabilitation in the Blue Ribbon Commission report, some sections had a very strong emphasis on offender-oriented behavior modification. The report in its entirety makes clear a commitment to a multipurpose and "balanced" approach to punishment accountability. But misunderstandings could have been avoided if the details given to prevention and behavior modification approaches had been set against more details about retributive and denunciatory aspects of "public protection." This combination would have provided a more "balanced" philosophical framework for subsequent policy discussions.

3

Getting Tough on Crime

To understand the current interest in intermediate sanctions, it is necessary to understand the penal debate about the purposes of sentencing and the assumption made about our primary form of punishment, the prison. Frustrated rehabilitators have emerged to lead the prison reductionist movement. They are inspired by a belief that prisons are either "uncivilized" or counterproductive as correctional institutions and should be used as little as possible. This belief is not, in principle, incompatible with the more sophisticated denunciatory-retributive sentencing philosophy that emerged from the back-to-justice era. Punishment was always supposed to be graded and related to the degree of wrongful behavior. Paying the penalty in the coinage of restricted liberty can be priced according to the seriousness of the crime. Logically, in addition to the loss of imprisonment measured in days, weeks, months, and years, there exists the possibility of extending the tariff into community settings. There is no reason why there should not be a range of supervised restrictions on an offender's liberty in the community.

Hence, there was by 1990 in California intellectual support for the idea of intermediate sanctions. But penal reforms need more than just a good idea (Chapter 5). There must be a practical aspect to interest administrators in an innovation. Administrations and governments will not wish to expose themselves to the risks involved in the politically sensitive field of sentencing policy. Nor will they seek to face the costs or the re-organizational battles required, unless there is a belief that there is a practical advantage.

By 1990 in California, the pragmatic and the philosophical support for intermediate sanction coincided. The pragmatic commitment to sentencing reform came about as a result of the consequences of the unprecedented expansion of the California criminal justice system during the 1980s. In 1988 a survey (Davies, 1989) was conducted among Californian criminal justice officials to determine how they had adjusted to the rapidly expanding system, to see what problems they were having, and in particular how they had adjusted to the resource constraint of jail and prison capacity limitations at a time when ever-increasing numbers of offenders were coming into the system, and politicians and the public were making ever more demands on it. The resulting chaos led to demands for a more systematic, comprehensive, and structured system of justice to achieve a better balance in which the resources available matched the demands made on them, a system in which the goals were clarified to allow for a more coherent and balanced approach to the issues of crime and justice.

"DISJOINTED EXPANSIONISM" IN CALIFORNIA

"The criminal justice system in California defies easy formulation. But even those twelve blind men who in their endeavor to describe the elephant ended up with twelve separate accounts of twelve separate parts would not have failed to notice that the beast was getting bigger" (Davies, 1988a, p. 1). The volume of crime reports, arrests, criminal filings, prosecutions, court cases, and offenders sentenced increased; manpower and budgets of the agencies responsible for law enforcement, prosecution, and incarceration swelled; the caseloads of parole and probation officers overwhelmed them; new jails and prisons proliferated.

By 1990 a quarter of a million meals were served each day in California state prisons, according to Jim Rowlands, the Director of the California Department of Corrections at that time. While there is little doubt about the magnitude of this change during the 1980s, what is in question is whether the enlarged penal estate will become the white elephant of the 1990s (i.e., a property requiring much care and expense and yielding little profit).

But the governor of California, George Deukmejian, had few doubts about the expansion of the criminal justice system. In January 1988 in his State of the State Address, he said, "Currently 35 percent of convicted felons are sent to state prisons. The remaining 65 percent receive alternative sentences" (Deukmejian, 1988). Governor Deukmejian's stance on alternatives to imprisonment was clear. "The remaining 65 percent receive alternative sentences. We should not consider further alternatives to incarceration, so long as there are hardened criminals who will not consider alternatives to crime" (1989). But while Governor Deukmejian resolved to stick with imprisonment as his major penal strategy, the counties, because of the financial burden of building and operating jails, turned in increasing numbers to electronic surveillance and home curfew as a refinement in the tariff of penalties available to the municipal and justices courts.

The cornerstone of penal policy in California since the Determinate Sentencing Law of 1976 has been imprisonment. In the context of a "law and order" culture, it seemed probable that this reform, which stressed punishment and sought greater uniformity, certainty and honesty in sentencing practice, was adding to the pressure to incarcerate more people.

The mystique of expertise provided an ideological barrier to public participation during the era of indeterminate sentencing. With the shift to punishment and "just deserts," the question of appropriate penalties opened up into a public auction of bids; and as in the way of auctions, the bids always went higher. After all, "deserved" punishment is not a matter of science; nor is it based on absolute or natural criteria but is a matter of judgment. More punitive judgments about deserved sentence lengths and false expectations about the protection provided by incarceration coalesced into campaigns for more mandatory and longer sentences.

The elected district attorneys and judges swept along by this mood respectively demanded and granted more jail and prison sentences. The use of imprisonment increased. At the same time, the system of discretionary parole release was abolished with the removal of the Adult Authority and with it a pragmatically useful safety valve with which to cope with prison overcrowding.

The expansion of the prison system during this era was inevitable. There have been seventeen major state prison building developments since 1983. In 1982, there were twelve state prisons; by 1992, there were twenty-three. The expansion continues. As of March 1, 1988 new bed capacity of state prisons was being expanded by 26,000 with 16,366 beds completed, and 10,000 more under construction. This is costing \$2.2 billion. An additional \$1.8 billion is required to build a further 21,000 beds, in part to be funded by the 1988 Bond Act. Vacaville now holds over 8,000 inmates and must rank among the list of largest prisons in the world.

The Bureau of Criminal Statistics' publication *Crime and Delinquency in California, 1980–1989* states that since 1980, the rate of adults under state supervision has almost tripled. In 1992, there were 190,187 adults per day under state supervision, with 104,352 in state institutions (23 prisons and 40 camps) and the rest, 85,835, on parole (Department of Corrections, 1992). By 1994 the Blue Ribbon Commission reports that the average daily state prison population of adults is projected to reach 136,000. In 1989, there were 359,000 adults under county or city supervision, with 74,000 in jail per day, 248,000 on probation and 40,000 awaiting trial. In 1988, Los Angeles County held on average 22,319 in its jails.

Criminal justice personnel grew in number by 35 percent between 1980 and 1989. By 1989, there were 137,759 full-time employees working in the state and local criminal justice agencies. Sixty percent (84,000) were in law enforcement, with 9,000 in prosecution agencies, 3,000 public defender agency personnel,

1,700 court staff, and 40,000 in state and local correctional agencies.

The number of employees at the Department of Corrections grew from 8,000 in 1982 to 30,767 in 1992. It is now a very different organization from the one led so successfully by Richard McGee in the era stretching from the 1940s to the 1960s. The Prison Construction and Planning Section of the CDC had one staff member in 1983; now there are 150. This section can now plan, build, and fill a prison in a very short time. With the growth of the CDC, new career opportunities open up for employees, but this is not without its potential dangers. When Avenal prison was opened in 1987, all of its supervisory and managerial staff from superintendent to lieutenants were new to their posts.

It is likely that prison costs will rise rather than fall. Staffing costs are critical in terms of the economics of operating a prison. By 1988, the guards' association, the California Correctional Peace Officers Association, had 17,000 members.

With more lawyers per head of population than anywhere else in the world, it is not surprising that prisoners act just like other Californians and turn to litigation to pursue their interests. Overcrowded jails and prisons lead to conditions that are considered unhygienic, cramped, and dangerous to inmates. The courts have put population limits on prisons and jails. The cost of employing a sufficient number of lawyers in the Department of Justice to handle litigation by inmates against the CDC was $5.25 million in 1988. This amount does not include the cost of hiring trial lawyers by the CDC, or the paralegals employed in its Compliance Division. In 1988, twenty-four counties had court-ordered population caps on their jails.

Despite this unprecedented buildup of the penal estate in California, the California Crime Index (CCI) increased between 1984–1990. As a proportion of its population, California imprisons four times as many citizens as does the United Kingdom, which does not have a separate system of local jails, and separate state and federal prisons. In 1990, the proportion of the adult population incarcerated in the United Kingdom was 100 to 100,000, compared with 440 to 100,000 in California (Bureau of Criminal Statistics, 1990, p. 90).

But the impact of imprisonment in terms of incapacitation, deterrence, and rehabilitation is far from certain. Crime has increased, in some cases dramatically. Drug arrests have risen by 97 percent during the five-year period from 1982 to 1987. The demands on the system will continue to grow as demographic pressures build. California's population is expected to increase by half a million individuals per year over the next decade. With this growth will come more crime and more prison inmates. The reliance on incarceration in California as the most favored response to the crime problem will require that even greater resources be spent on new prison construction to house record inmate numbers. What is certain is that projected inmate figures for state prisons will pass the 100,000 figure in the early 1990s; that the growth of new prison building will not match the projected growth in the use of imprisonment; and that prison construction and operations will be a major item of expenditure in the Californian state budget.

Of course, these trends are not restricted to California. In 1989 there were 4.1 million adults under the authority of correctional, parole, or probation officials across the United States. According to the U.S. Justice Department's Bureau of Justice Statistics (1990), in 1989 there was a 13 percent increase in the nation's prison population. John Irwin and James Austin wrote in 1987, "The United States has embarked on an unprecedented incarceration binge. Since the last decade our nation's prison population has more than doubled. Billions of dollars are being allocated to construct tens of thousands of new cells in a futile effort to catch up with the increasing prison populations. But despite this historic prison construction program, state prison systems will continue to be overcrowded" (p. 6). There are criminal justice officials in California who think there is no further explanation required than that provided by Irwin and Austin to account for the current interest in intermediate sanctions.

EXPANSION IN CALIFORNIA: SURVEY OF CRIMINAL JUSTICE OFFICIALS

In 1988 all chief probation officers, district attorneys, police chiefs in large cities, public defenders, sheriffs, and presiding judges of the appeal courts, superior courts, and municipal courts were sent a questionnaire about the growth of the criminal justice system in California.

Sponsored by the California Attorney General's Office, the survey was sent by mail to 420 individuals on February 22, 1988. The individuals included in the survey were "notables" in the local criminal justice agencies. State officials, employees, and state-level agencies were not included. The questionnaire and a letter of introduction were sent to presiding judges of the courts of appeal (18), presiding judges of the superior courts (58), presiding judges of municipal courts (93), district attorneys (58), sheriffs (58), chief probation officers (58), police chiefs in cities with populations over 100,000 (35) and to the public defenders in those counties that have a defender's office (40).

By July 1988, 294 replies had been received (i.e., 70 percent), a very high completion rate for a postal survey. Earl Babbie in *Survey Research Methods* (1973, p. 165) states that "a response rate of at least 50 percent is adequate for analysis and reporting. A response rate of at least 60 percent is good and a response rate of 70 percent or more is very good."

A comparison of the completion rate for the survey among the differing criminal justice functionaries shows a rate ranging from 59 to 79 percent: chief probation officers (79 percent), district attorneys (78 percent), police chiefs (77 percent), sheriffs (75 percent), public defenders (68 percent), presiding judges of the superior, municipal, and appeal courts (59 percent).

The survey was to elicit the views and attitudes of these key personnel within the criminal justice system on how the expansion of the 1980s had impacted the system in California. In particular, the survey sought views about the major administrative problems facing individual criminal justice agencies; the major changes over the 1980s decade; the extent of system awareness and interdependency between the various agencies; the perceived need for greater coordination; the identification of the tasks to be accomplished if greater coordination were desired; and who, if anyone, should be responsible for greater coordination.

The responses to the survey indicated wide variations between the agencies and the counties in the perceptions of the way the system was working. But a cross-agency and cross-state consensus emerged on two issues. First, there was agreement on the growth in the volume of work and the associated problem of insufficient resources. Second, there was a shared concern about the inadequate public awareness and understanding of the work of the criminal justice agencies.

There was a sufficient number of comments from across the agencies and counties to conclude that more than a few respondents felt uneasy with a system that was driven in some cases less by the concern for the public safety and justice and more by the weight of numbers in the system. It is worth recalling that these comments about "chaos" and "inefficiencies" were not offered by headline-seeking journalists or by "bleeding heart liberals" who shudder at the mention of incarceration, but by experienced professionals from within the system who run the agencies and preside over the courts.

The impact of growth on the organizational arrangements of one agency was made clear by the district attorney from a middle-sized county who wrote: "Our office has grown in style so that informal and day-to-day communication is a luxury of the past. Informal management styles are inappropriate to present-day demands. Handling problems as they develop without anticipating budgetary, personnel and technical needs generally results in an inadequate resolution. In short, our entire management approach has changed" (Davies, 1988a, p. 7).

Many of the statements—in particular those expressed by the district attorneys, police, sheriffs, and municipal court judges—showed that at least some of the agencies sought to be self-regulating in light of the impact on other agencies struggling with resource constraints. Most frequently mentioned was the jail-space limitation in the sheriff's department. Agencies and courts were adjusting decisions in recognition of systemic resource realities. System capacity imposes an inexorable logic on all participants, resulting in enhanced interagency sensitivity and even self-regulation.

Abraham Blumberg (1967) describes the work of a metropolitan court system that under the pressure of numbers is geared to production, which achieves a self-regulating equilibrium at the expense of due process and justice by the mechanism of plea negotiation with each actor in the system—except the naive defendant—playing their role in this production line model to achieve the efficient, in bureaucratic terms, processing of cases. Blumberg wrote about the court system in New York, but his analysis has relevance to West Coast justice.

High profile cases might still embody the ideals of due process, but the routine cases clearly involve, and have always involved, the cooperation of a variety of criminal justice agencies and the courts in an unwritten agreement to "do the business." At least one superior court judge thought that the volume of business had resulted in goal displacement, "Plea bargaining and sentence bargaining have become custom and practice of settling cases without regard to anything except coping with the volume of cases." There is a "total disregard for the protection of the public as a legitimate end of the criminal justice system" (Davies, 1988a, p. 17).

In most systems there are informal aspects of the process that allow the demands made on the system to adjust to the limited resources of time, manpower and facilities. This allows the system's principles to be maintained even when they are not regularly achieved in practice. Trial by jury, though available to all felony defendants, accounted for only 7 percent of felony dispositions in 1987. In 1977, when the determinate sentencing laws came into force, trials were held in 15 percent of felony case dispositions. The negotiation over the charge and the sentence length is the key to this process of self-regulation in the criminal justice system. But in California the room for maneuver has been drastically curtailed since 1976 through the introduction of the determinate sentencing law and the increasing use of mandatory sentences. Furthermore, plea bargaining in serious felony cases and for the offense of driving while under the influence of alcohol or drugs was banned by a voters' initiative in 1982.

There has been a quantum leap in the size of the system in California. It seems likely that with this growth has come an enhanced agency awareness of the needs of the system because of the number of cases and a larger volume of work. The impact of the higher volume of business and the problems associated with it has been defused in part by the arrival of agency-specific computers and data bases. This ability to handle more cases could paradoxically lead to greater coordination problems in the future due to the incompatibility of information systems.

The complications associated with this quantum leap are beginning to show. Not all parts of the system expanded at the optimum rate in terms of system consequences. In this respect, the police are crucial as frontline definers and gatekeepers of the inflow into the system. From 1981 to 1986 the adult felony arrest rate increased by 21 percent. The consequent expansion exposed the county jails and state prisons to litigation and court-dictated population limits. In effect, this is a further manifestation of the major constraint on the expansion of the system resources. How can the system cope, given that resources are limited and that they might become more scarce? Demand on the system is likely to rise even more as a result of a state population that grew by nearly 9 million people between 1981 and 1991. Some agencies and courts have already achieved much in the way of improved efficiency through organizational reforms and experiments to reduce costs. Governor Deukmejian announced his view that the state prisons can yet become more cost-effective through the use of prison labor. But the potential for agency-specific efficiencies is limited, so that the solution has to be sought by either improving coordination within the system to achieve greater efficiency or by reducing the demands on the system.

In California, to reduce the demands on the criminal justice system requires a change in outlook among the voters. It is an electorate-led process of decision making, controlled in part by ballot initiatives that can impose detailed and specific policies on the criminal justice system, for example, the initiative adopted in June 1988 that led to a change in the sentence for the second degree murder of a law officer. The periodic election of sheriffs, judges, district attorneys as well as politicians also ensures a voter-led approach to criminal justice reforms. One district attorney thought that somebody should "confront and educate the public on whether it is in the public's interest to keep incarcerating larger numbers of people at enormous cost and diversion of scare resources from other social goals" (Davies, 1988a, p. 8).

The shift to tougher sentencing policy with the advent of determinate sentencing laws was identified as was a recognition of the "law and order" culture of contemporary California. Public opinion has changed, states one police chief, from "anti law-enforcement to pro law-enforcement" (Davies, 1988a, p. 7). A similar recognition of this mood was expressed differently by one public defender, "lock'em up and throw away the key is as politically popular as God and Motherhood, not to mention apple pie" (1988a, p. 7).

Bringing about changes in the political culture would involve a long-term effort to improve public education about the nature of the system and the opportunity costs that exist within the system. The 1988 survey found a strong strand of support for this approach. A majority believed that the system was both overpoliticized and too dependent on shifts in public opinion. Many felt the public lacked an awareness and understanding of the problems of the agencies. A clear majority agreed with the proposal to survey public knowledge of the system and introduce efforts to promote better understanding of the costs, conditions, and consequences of the justice and penal systems. In a democracy "we must educate our Masters," Disraeli recommended. In late twentieth-century California it is the media, more than the schools, that could provide this understanding if they chose to improve the quality and comprehension of their coverage of criminal justice issues.

In the meantime, some solutions are already being found. The survey reveals that there is experimentation. Electronic surveillance and non-custodial alternatives, reluctantly accepted by some, are being used in place of jail. Seventeen counties in 1988 were experimenting with electronic surveillance as an alternative to jail. Privatization of criminal justice is creeping into the system in some counties in California, not in the form of private jails but through the electronic monitoring that some agencies rely on to provide the morning computer printout to identify infringements of the home curfew rules.

New technology would appear to be making inroads in two ways: (1) as a means to cope with the routines and everyday procedure within organizations; and (2) to pioneer new procedures made possible by the new technology. Over the past two years in Glendale the police have been experimenting with a video arraignment system with a local courthouse. "This reduces in-custody movement, makes for quicker, easier court disposition and reduces the chances of escape," commented the chief of police (Davies, 1988a, p. 7). Sheriffs' departments and probation services throughout the state are experimenting with electronic surveillance and monitoring.

Other realities emerged that helped the agencies to adapt to the pressure of caseloads, and the related problems of inadequate resources and legal intervention. Diversion from custody or alternatives to incarceration were reluctantly introduced at the county level as a spontaneous response to the practical emergencies of overcrowding. Work-in-lieu, work furlough, home confinement, and electronic surveillance were all adding to the range of options for the local criminal justice system. Ideologically justified in terms of a work ethic and greater surveillance, they were an unplanned response to a crisis of funding and court-capped jail populations. This exosmotic process, so called because it represents a flow from the inside of a system to the outside and from one area of high concentration to one of lower concentration, was a pragmatic response without the benefit of prolonged deliberation among the policy makers. It has resulted in a refinement of the "tariffs" available to the sentencing judge for misdemeanor offenses.

This new penalty system has not undergone much in the way of systematic evaluation other than passing the test of being comparatively cheaper than jail. The effect this has is unsettling and unclear, according to some of the comments made in the survey by district attorneys, sheriffs, and police chiefs. It adds to the uncertainty in the system and might well turn out to be unfair in terms of the uniformity required by statute in respect to determinate sentencing practice. The exosmotic process is undoubtedly a reflection of a spontaneous adaptation within the system, but this self-leveling is a response to resource deficiencies rather than a concern with justice or public protection. It is another indication of the lack of system awareness and *discorrespondence* in the system. It is a system that seems bereft of cooperation and coordination, and can best be described as ad hoc.

The concern, however, with this ad hoc approach is that it will lead to even more disparities between counties in the way they respond to law breaking and offenders. One public defender commented, "In Los Angeles a person is given probation whereas in Madera he is sent to state prison" (Davies, 1988a, p. 19). Ad hoc experimentation does not guarantee that good practice in one jurisdiction is disseminated to other counties, or that impractical innovations are monitored.

The assimilation of ad hoc arrangements is not a problem in a system that is stable or evolving slowly. Political analysts use the term *disjointed incrementalism* to describe the steady but unplanned growth of government bureaucracies. However, the 1980s were an expansionist era in California's penal history, an expansion made possible by a political and judicial system that was markedly responsive to electoral concerns about law and order. The subsequent expansion was unsystematic, unplanned, and ad hoc in nature. It was not disjointed incrementalism but disjointed expansionism. The invisible hand of bureaucratic intervention within the courts, which allowed for self-regulating equilibrium according to Blumberg, (1967) was swamped and unable to cope with the volume of business. More hands—visible hands—were needed. The courts were overwhelmed not only by the volume of cases but by the increase in complexity of handling criminal cases and the greater rigidity resulting from the determinate sentencing laws.

PRISON CAPACITY AND COSTS: ITS IMPACT ON CRIMINAL JUSTICE DECISIONS

The survey's reference to improving the coordination of the criminal justice system in California was interpreted by some respondents as a threat to the constitutional principles of the separation of powers and the due process of law. A response from one district attorney's office articulated the following points about the survey.

> It is misleading to analyze California's criminal justice system in other than the most general manner. No detailed analysis of such a system is likely to be productive because no such system exists. Rather, the agencies that this survey groups together are independent systems themselves and the agencies are not designed to cooperate with the other agencies to reach a common goal—or at least the common goals implied in this survey.
>
> Police-prosecution agencies have common goals and these agencies cooperate to achieve such goals. Criminal defense agencies (and the private criminal defense bar) and the courts do not cooperate to achieve common goals with the prosecution-police agencies, other than to follow the procedures of the courts in the prosecution of criminal defendants.
>
> Legal tradition and constitutional law in the United States provide that the system to prosecution shall be *adversary*, rather than cooperative or inquisitorial. Because of the 5th and 6th Amendments the defendant and his attorney are independent of the courts and prosecution and owe no duties

> of cooperation into the investigation of crime. Although since *Mapp v. Ohio* the courts have increasingly regulated practically all aspects of prosecution. Nonetheless, neither the prosecution agencies nor the courts can be termed an arm of the other as perhaps in some European systems. Each agency is protected by the doctrine of separation of powers. (Davies, 1988a, p. 11–12).

Some observers of government in the United States regard the fragmentation and lack of cooperation and coordination as an inevitable consequence of a system built upon the principle of separation of the powers of government. The checks and balances in the system exist to protect the liberty of the citizen, and if this results in a lack of common purpose, operational inefficiency, and dysfunctional consequences, then so be it.

There is clearly unease felt by those with judicial responsibilities for any policy reform that might appear to blur the distinction between the judiciary and the executive branch of government. The use of the term *coordination* in the survey was not intended to undermine the principles of the separation of powers of government.

However, the political realities of the world make it difficult to regard constitutional principles as absolutes standing in splendid isolation from the world's realities. There is another constitutional principle, the rule of law by which policies can be legitimately changed if proper constitutional procedures are followed. This tension is reflected in the contradiction expressed by the layman who simultaneously "wants the government off his back" but thinks that "there ought to be a law about it"—"it" being the latest public concern of the citizenry. In short, constitutional principles are guides to the fundamental values of a society, but they are unlikely to be the only values of a society.

The principle of the due process of law is recognized as a vital aspect of civil liberties in democratic societies. For the individual accused of a crime, the due process of law permits a public hearing in court. The due process of law does not guarantee fairness; but its absence would almost certainly result in less fairness. The independence of the judiciary plays a crucial part in this procedure.

Societies may shift the balance between the polarities of the "control model" and the "due process model" of law enforcement. One district attorney in the survey thought that there had been a shift in this balance over the last ten years. He wrote:

> The most fundamental change has been the incredible proliferation of defendant's rights and the resulting complexity that this superimposes on the criminal justice system. This has made the prosecutor's job so hard that it is often very difficult for a very skilled prosecutor to know what to do in a given situation. . . . This complexity greatly increases the length of time necessary to get a case to trial and then to try it. When I began as a prosecutor nineteen years ago, a preliminary hearing took 15 to 30 minutes in most cases. Today a preliminary on the same type of case can easily take two hours. (Davies, 1988a, p. 12)

This extract is not quoted to elicit a yearning for the good old days of "Justice Without Trial" (Skolnick, 1974) but to point out that increasing the defendant's rights extends the length of time of trial and increases the procedural complexities so that an increase in resources is required to deal with the same number of cases.

Should resource considerations be taken into account when the issue of justice is concerned? The reality is that resources do influence the judgments and decisions of officials in the criminal justice system. As the survey shows, resources affect police work, prosecution decisions and judicial sentencing. Reflecting a frustration with resource constraints, a municipal court judge complained, "Just tell us judges the extent to which our decisions will be negated by influences and limitations beyond our control. The degree to which a criminal judge can function has largely become the province of correctional facilities" (Davies, 1988a, p. 12).

As Table 3.1 shows, the majority of respondents (59 percent) maintain that prison overcrowding at the back end of the system affects decisions made throughout the system. Some agencies are more influenced than others by the cost of incarceration, but still 37 percent maintained that it had an impact. Of the 289 respondents, 101 (35 percent) said that neither costs nor overcrowding had affected decisions. To clarify the nature of this influence, a follow-up question asked the respondents to describe in their own words "in what way does it have an impact?" It was clear from their answers that individual cases and operational decisions were affected.

Table 3.1
Impact of Prison and Jail Costs and Overcrowding: Does it Influence Decisions? (Total Replies: 289)

	Yes	No	Don't Know
Does the cost of incarceration have any impact on decisions made by you and your colleagues?	37%	62%	1%
Does the current level of overcrowding in jails and prisons have any impact on decisions made by you and your colleagues?	59%	38%	3%

(*Source*: Davies, 1988b)

How the Individual Agencies Responded

Sheriffs. The Sheriffs' departments were affected in more ways than the other agencies: fiscal concern about the resources for jails and personnel; court-capped limits on jail populations; need to build new jails; search for alternative programs; the problem of where to house inmates; manpower deployment decisions; early release of inmates; pretrial booking decisions; electronic surveillance experiments; and difficult choices to make in respect to the operational decisions affecting investigation and law enforcement. As one sheriff wrote, it "affects virtually every decision" (p. 13). Another admitted, "Multitudes of operational decisions are impacted, the most basic being whether or not to even arrest an individual. Pending the financing and construction of adequate facilities to house prisoners, we spend our time finding ways to take prisoners out of jail when in fact they should stay in jail" (p. 13).

Four sheriffs wrote of being under a court compliance order to reduce their jail populations, and three referred to federal decrees. Four more wrote about the fear of lawsuits, and one maintained that litigation prevention had become the priority. "We do not have beds or housing to provide the minimum standards. Court-mandated requirements and the cost of lawsuits is causing devastation in the local community" (p. 13). Altogether twenty-four counties in California in 1988 were operating with court-ordered population limits on their jails.

Four described their jail construction program, and others mentioned the way the expansion of jail populations and costs was eating into their law enforcement budget. "Getting through each fiscal year" had become the goal of one department. Four departments mentioned the increased use of alternatives to incarceration, but one commented, "We are bound to take many steps to alleviate overcrowding. Such decisions do not necessarily serve the end of justice" (p. 13).

Most worrying to some sheriffs (8) was that the extra resources required for dealing with the jail problem were coming from law enforcement activities, with correspondingly less manpower for patrols and investigations. Arrest decisions were affected, "My patrolmen are discouraged from making public intoxication arrests" (p. 13). Six sheriffs' departments utilize an early-release policy for offenders, typically petty criminals and drunk drivers. Clearly some imagination has gone into the development of alternatives to incarceration and number juggling.

Police. "We are impacted by agencies who do allow overcrowding to affect their decisions even though we don't, " commented one police chief (p. 13). Another chief complained of the way resources had influenced other agencies, "Neither the cost of incarceration nor the lack of space for incarceration deters us from performing our duties as aggressively as necessary. Unfortunately, some components of the criminal justice system have adopted the posture that they should diminish their activities in deference to further problems along the criminal justice line" (p. 14). These two views were not typical of the opinions expressed by most of the police departments. Of the twenty-seven replies from police departments in cities with a population of 100,000 or more, only ten maintained that costs and overcrowding made no difference. Fifteen said overcrowding in jails had influenced decisions in their departments.

Many comments focused on the impact on arrests and booking procedures, especially the increased use of citations and release rather than custody for misdemeanors. "It causes us all to rethink our priorities in terms of arrests, especially deploying task forces or special enforcement units to put down a particular problem. If you have no room at the inn you shouldn't arrest, is kind of the order of the day" (p. 14). Another commented, "Basically it means there is no detention of misdemeanants" (p. 14).

The policy of other agencies can directly affect the work of the police. "When county jails refuse acceptance of prisoners charged with offenses which do not meet their criteria for confinement, alternatives are necessary" (p. 14). Some pressure is less direct, "The jail early release program subconsciously affects an officer's desire to arrest some types of people. The same people are arrested multiple times due to the early release program" (p. 14). Recognition of the revolving door syndrome was clearly spelled out in the Blue Ribbon Report of 1990. Other pressure comes from recognition of the agency interdependency within the system, "political pressure to avoid new or more effective enforcement programs, due to the inability of the county to staff the district attorney's office, the courts or provide jail space" (p. 14).

District Attorneys. "The overcrowding issue is being used as an excuse to unfairly cut sentences. Overcrowding of jails and prisons is a problem caused by criminals and we must stop acting like it's caused by prosecution, police officers and taxpayers" (p. 14). This comment reveals one district attorney's frustration and yet recognition that overcrowding does affect decisions in the system. The majority of district attorneys (27) thought that either costs or overcrowding had an impact, while nineteen thought they did not.

Some of the district attorneys were ready to point the finger at other agencies which they thought were influenced by the overcrowding and costs of incarceration. In particular, they identified judges and sheriffs. District attorneys thought that overcrowding and costs led to greater leniency in pretrial decisions, such as bail, sometimes with undesirable consequences. "Although there is more pressure to agree to lesser sentences, the real impact is where a defendant is released due to overcrowding and doesn't show up and when he's picked up he may be released again" (p. 14). These two factors influenced the decision of whether or not to prosecute an individual. "It creates an insidious pressure to refuse prosecution of non-violent offenders in order to maintain jail space for the serious non-violent offenders" (p. 14). Reduction in sentence lengths and less use of custodial dispositions were mentioned, typically, "We have severe overcrowding. . . . We often find ourselves unable to ask for jail, in cases in which we would routinely do so" (p. 14).

Decisions are self-adjusted to the realities of the system. "In the evaluation of cases and in negotiating case dispositions we are always mindful of what a court might do if the parties fail to reach accord. We are impressed that sentencing practice is becoming more liberal because of financial and space considerations" (p. 14). Part of the self-adjustment arises from the constraint imposed by court-ordered population limits, for example, "Our jail is under a consent decree limiting bed space. Release decisions and sentence choices reflect this constriction" (p. 14).

While the constraint of available jail space is regarded by several district attorneys as allowing for more "liberal" sentences and "alternatives," two comments suggested that this same pressure can encourage the use of state imprisonment and longer terms. "Because the county has a jail population cap imposed by a federal court order, there is great pressure on the DA and judge to impose minimum jail sentences, particularly on convicted misdemeanants; to find alternatives to jail sentences; and to give prison sentences to the more serious offenders, thus creating bed space in the county jail" (p. 15). Passing on the inmate housing problem to the state is also shown by the following statement, "We try to avoid lengthy incarceration in the county jail which is under a federal court order. We therefore seek home confinement or state prison as alternatives" (p. 15).

Public Defenders. Public defenders are less directly affected by the resource constraint, but eight thought it did affect other agencies so that "the local sheriff asks for more freedom than the public defender" (p. 15). Two public defenders though that prison sentences were sometimes given instead of a term in county jail because of overcrowding. One commented, "The judges now send more defendants to prison because local jail space is limited" (p. 15).

Jail crowding and costs can influence public defenders' decisions in that they strengthen their negotiating hand when plea-bargaining with the district attorney or asking for pretrial release. As one defender euphemistically phrased it, "We cooperate with other agencies to reduce overcrowding" (p. 15).

Probation. One-third of chief probation officers replied that the cost and crowding in jails and prison had no impact on the decisions made by their departments, but two-thirds thought it did. The search for alternatives to incarceration involved probation departments in heavy caseloads and even caused some inappropriate commitments to probation.

Eighteen of the forty-six respondents maintained that costs and overcrowding influenced the sentence recommendations made by their departments, while the trend indicated by most replies was the search for, and use of, non-custodial alternatives (14) or recommending shorter jail terms. Two chief probation officers expressed concern about the inappropriate use of prison sentences for some offenders. One commented that, "we send more to prison that may have been placed on probation if adequate resources were available" (p. 15). This is a costly alternative for the state taxpayer with the average cost per inmate in state prison at $17,000 per year [in 1988], not to mention the impact on the individual offender caught up in the pressure to send the long-term jail cases to prison.

While two comments implied a rationing process and utilizing incarceration for those dangerous to the public, one commentator suggested that overcrowding permits the early release of dangerous offenders.

Judges. The presiding judges of the courts of appeal were not influenced by the resource implications of overcrowded and costly jails and prisons. One offered the view, "I am an appeal judge, I suspect decisions on the trial level probably are affected" (p. 15). Another judge offered the view that, "no judge can be totally unaffected by the crowded jails and prisons and the exorbitant expense to the taxpayer" (p. 16).

The majority of presiding judges in the superior court claimed not to be affected by overcrowding or the cost of incarceration. Ten admitted that these two factors came into their consideration of pretrial and sentencing choices. One commented, "The overcrowding has a direct impact on some sentencing decisions. If the jail is overcrowded, some people who might be sentenced to jail will probably be placed on probation" (p. 15). Another judge wrote, "We must develop creative methods to eliminate the need to consider overcrowding as a decisional factor" (p. 16). A third commented, "I take it into account particularly with first-time or youthful offenders" (p. 16).

Alternative sentences previously reserved for less serious offenders are sought and utilized for more serious offenders; sentences are suspended. "Careful consideration is given to the value of incarceration as a punishment. It is often weighed against the hazard to custodial personnel and fellow inmates, particularly with respect to non-violent crimes; crimes of violence and high impact crime such as drug sales are rarely if ever affected by overcrowding considerations" (p. 16).

Of the fifty-seven presiding judges of the municipal courts, forty-four (77 percent) agreed that overcrowding affected their decisions. Eight denied that it had an impact. While the majority (31) maintained that costs did not have an impact, others (21) thought it did. Over half of all the presiding judges (55 percent) thought that overcrowding in jails and prisons affected decisions, and 30 percent believed that the cost of incarceration had an impact on themselves and their colleagues. Even when the judges believed that offenders deserved incarceration, the resource implications outweighed the preferred solution. "If I sent to jail every person that I really feel deserves jail time and for the length of time I feel they should remain, and if my colleagues did the same, we would need a much larger facility" (p. 16).

DEMANDS FOR A SYSTEMS APPROACH

The problems of the penal system are not just a matter of managing an expensive resource. Prisons are at the back end of a process in which those who run the prisons have little or no control over the demand for prison places and cannot restrict or regulate the numbers that are sent to them. Decisions are made primarily at the front end of the process by those who enforce the law (police and prosecutors), by those who define the law (legislators), and by those who adjudicate on the law in the courts (judges).

There is no mechanism similar to market forces at work as in other unregulated markets to bring about equilibrium between the supply of and the demand for scare resources. In this case the invisible hand is invisible because there are no resource allocation mechanisms of any form to be seen.

The lack of systematic regulation of the criminal justice system is applauded by those who regard it as a manifestation of the separation of powers principle. There is a strong argument in a democratic society for having separate organizations be responsible for the judicial, executive, and legislative functions of government. The liberty of the citizenry is less likely to be threatened by a system of government That is based on the principle of the separation of powers.

But the defense of the separation of powers principle should not blind us to the realities of a criminal justice system in which informal and unofficial regulation already exists and political concerns shape administrative and judicial decisions. We should be wary of those who mask their concern about loss of power as an issue of separation of powers, and we must be aware that this principle will be used to legitimate the fragmentation in the system of government—a fragmentation that might be less a product of the separation of powers principle and more a result of historic arrangements, established interests, and political inertia.

The reluctance to adopt a "whole system" approach is at the root of many of the problems of the criminal justice system. Ohlin and Remington (1958) exhorted us to understand that, "There is inadequate awareness of the fact that the administration of criminal justice is a single, total process and that, therefore, changing one important aspect may require substantial reorientation of the entire system" (p. 495). We need to build into our models of criminal justice not just due process and crime control considerations, but also the resource, organizational and administrative factors that shape decisions in the system.

Why should prison usage not be subject to policy prioritization, given limited resources, in the same way schools and hospitals are? If "life-opportunity" choices provided by educational and medical policy decisions are subject to resource constraints, then why not sentencing decisions? A more comprehensive and systematic approach to prison use requires first and foremost closer monitoring and control over sentencing decisions. Judges in Britain resist this idea. But as Lord Hutchinson (1988) points out, "Judicial isolation is not the same as judicial independence. . . . It is not self-evident that the separation of powers carries the implication that sentencing policy is a matter solely for judges" (p. 40).

The gap between myths and facts has been successfully narrowed in the last twenty years, as empirically oriented criminologists have recorded what actually happens in the system of justice, as opposed to what is supposed to happen. It was not apparent from these studies that defendants were treated as if innocent until proven guilty, that plea negotiations were something that happened elsewhere, that disparities in sentencing did not exist, and that prosecution and judgments were immune from ideological and resource influences.

Myths, facts, and resources help to influence decisions about the criminal justice system, but it is a system only in the sense of being a process through which defendants are filtered. In other respects there is a lack of system awareness, especially in a resource and planning sense. The authors of the Blue Ribbon Commission report wrote eloquently in California that:

> The criminal justice system in California is out of balance and will remain so unless the entire state and local criminal justice system is addressed from prevention through discharge of jurisdiction. . . .
>
> State and local corrections must be viewed as a system in developing corrections policy. Prison overcrowding is contributed to by probation underfunding and jail overcrowding and underfunding. The corrections system is presently lacking sufficient integrated strategies to manage probation, jail and prison populations. (Blue Ribbon Commission, p. 4)

The historic arrangements associated with the enactment of the California Penal Code in 1872 were a reflection of an era when the counties were the natural unit of administration in a state where the people were scattered across wide distances, living in predominantly rural areas or small towns, with poor transportation and slow communications. A decentralized system was needed for an essentially localized criminal justice system. The majority of Californians no longer have a rural, small-town life-style. Today more than three quarters of them live in four sprawling conurbations: Los Angeles, San Diego, Sacramento, and the Bay area. Today's Californians are more mobile than ever before, and the social, economic, and political issues that concern them are less likely to fit into the jurisdictional boundaries of the county system. The state versus county tension is evident in many aspects of social and economic policy, such as education, welfare, and transportation. A highly educated and mobile populace is less likely to see the advantages of local autonomy when services are unevenly delivered and impeded by a fragmented administrative system.

The problems of fragmentation are considerable in California, where fifty-eight counties manifest very diverse criminal justice systems. These counties vary in size of population. The biggest is Los Angeles with 8 million people; the smallest Alpine County with a population of just over 1,000. They vary in style. They vary in size of organization. A telephone call to one sheriff's office led to the following dialogue with the receptionist, "Are you the sheriff's secretary?" "I'm the nearest thing he's got to a secretary." Some counties resent state interference, although to survive financially they have come to rely on state funding.

If you put this administrative fragmentation and parochialism into the political context of a state legislature in which the impact of new criminal justice policy is less important than is appearing to be tough on crime, with a cultural agenda set by a media with a preference for the sensational in crime coverage, and where the sheriffs, prosecutors, and judges are elected by the voters, you have the recipe for a short-term, unplanned, and uncoordinated response to the next panic about crime. Add to this the realization that despite the recent expansion of the system, the crime problem has not been solved, and the public's anxiety about crime continues.

Within the criminal justice system, interagency rivalry—even hostility—is not unknown. This rivalry is legitimized in part by the variations in tasks undertaken by the differing agencies, by professional ideologies, and by the principle of the separation of powers. It is also a consequence of the part played by a particular agency in the adversarial process of justice. This rivalry, in the context of multiple law enforcement and correctional agencies, with bureaucratic boundaries determined by the jurisdictional limits of the county line, and the competition for funds, results in a system in which agencies do not always effectively communicate or cooperate with each other. It is a system that can be described by the term *discorrespondent*, a term that conveys the impression that regular communication does not always exist between the agencies, and furthermore suggests that the parts do not always correspond or fit together.

For the naive offender who goes in one end and out of the other, the perception is of a system of law enforcement and punishment. In economic terms there is considerable interdependency, for one agency's output will be another agency's input. The public surely expect the police, prosecutors, judges, and correction agencies to be working as if they have a common task and coordinate their efforts toward that task. But within the agencies the professionals and managers who run them keep to keen boundaries of responsibility and jurisdiction. While performing differing tasks, they are entitled to retain a separate professional and organizational identity. But as part of a broader process and common purpose, surely their role also requires a degree of integration of effort into a wider system.

That the police are the frontline definers of the official process is not disputed, and that the inmate might "flow" through to a back-end acquaintance with a parole officer is true. What is in dispute is what degree of jurisdictional freedom should be retained regardless of the resource implications. To deny the resource implication of the process would be utopian, ignoring the unofficial self-regulation that already exists.

Contested trials before a jury are costly. Between 1985 and 1986, criminal cases rose by 18 percent in California superior courts. In terms of the flow and cost of cases, only 7 percent of criminal cases resulted in trial. Guilty pleas make the process organizationally and financially tenable. Yet if the courts saw a return to the 17 percent disposition by trial that existed before the Determinate Sentencing Law was introduced in 1977, the delay and cost would be unthinkable.

The counties in particular are squeezed between the policy makers in the state capital, Sacramento, and the police who define operationally which laws will be effectively enforced through the deployment of manpower. Sixty-one percent of police manpower is under the administrative control of the cities, whereas 80 percent of the prosecution costs and court costs are borne by the counties.

Some would regard it as disgraceful that the sentencing process should have to take into account the resource consequences of its work. That at the level of the individual case before the court the judge should be allowed within policy and statutory limits to make whatever choice of sentence seems most appropriate. But at the system level, resources will inevitably be taken into account. This can either be done informally and haphazardly or consciously and officially and be part of the policy-based limits on dispositions from the courts. So who is to decide and on whose advice?

Whether or not the political aspect of the problem can be solved is unclear. What is clear is that the economics of crime and punishment are already causing the state to pay for the criminal justice and penal agencies run by the counties, which are financially debilitated by Proposition 13 and the Gann Amendment.

Reform of the criminal justice and penal system is not to be justified by whether it brings about longer or shorter sentences for offenders, but by whether it can provide a greater rationality for the decision about the jurisprudential, political and social consideration as to the distribution of punishment. Reform should be justified by whether it promotes a more systematic and coordinated approach to sentencing policy by addressing the costs, conditions, and consequences of all the agencies involved in the system.

Exacerbated by economic uncertainties, policy shifts, and excessive numbers, one solution is to look for greater coordination throughout the system. The question then and now is "what form is coordination to take?"

The 1988 survey in California was based on the belief that the system would benefit from improved coordination and sought the views of "notables" within the system as to how the system might be improved. The responses to the questionnaire were to pinpoint perceived weaknesses in the system. The answers provided a range of ideas as to how improvement might be achieved. Equally important, the survey tested the "strength of feeling" about the alternative proposals to improve coordination suggested in the questionnaire.

The use of the term *coordination* did not imply one specific proposal for the reform of the system in California, but it did encourage a system-wide approach to solving problems. Coordination is defined as, "To place or arrange things in proper position relatively to each other and to the system of which they form parts; to bring into proper combined order as aspects of a whole" (*Oxford English Dictionary*).

Coordination in the criminal justice system can take many forms. A low-key form might involve greater liaison, consultation, and deliberation. It could lead to improved communications and cooperation between the agencies. It might involve more detailed monitoring of existing agencies and establishing clearer guidelines for prosecution and sentencing. It might take the form of regulating and rationing scarce and expensive state resources and limiting the availability of places in state prisons. Some officials would like to see aspects of the county system merged into regional or statewide organizations. Respondents' suggestions from the survey include: a statewide probation service, a statewide court system, a reduced number of law-enforcement agencies, amalgamation of jails and prisons under one body, and a merger between the probation and parole services.

There is clearly disagreement as to whether it is possible to talk about criminal justice in California in terms of a system. One of the pilot surveys was returned with the comment that the question about the features of the criminal justice system "cannot be analyzed as a whole in this manner as these (the response) categories apply to some parts but not to others" (p. 9). It was my expectation that some respondents would hesitate at this question and express the view that there was no California system of criminal justice. A sheriff commented, "It is a joke to call the criminal justice system a system. A system is several units or parts working together to achieve a common purpose, and it supports itself. Our system seems preoccupied with each unit defending its own position and blaming the other for failures of the system" (p. 11). However, as it turned out, most respondents felt able to express a system-wide view.

Strong views were expressed about the dysfunctional nature of the system and examples given of inadequate communication, non-cooperation, rivalry, even hostility between the agencies, "turf issues" and cross-purposes, non-existent planning and consolidation, and short-term crisis management that resulted in "chaos."

The general problem of the fragmentation and complexity of the administrative-political structure of California was captured in comments by an agency head in Tulare County, "By necessity Tulare County is required to conduct business dealings with special districts, cities, counties, California and other states and the federal government. The absence of a single agency which transcends political boundaries leads to bureaucratic delays and misunderstanding" (p. 10). Added to this administrative fragmentation is the excessive number of policing agencies. According to one sheriff, there are "too many law enforcement agencies at the state level, State Police, California Highway Patrol, State Parks, Alcoholic Beverage Control, Bureau of Narcotics Enforcement, etc." (p. 10).

The 1988 survey found strong support for improving the process of consultation on the impact of policy innovations. The impact of new laws and policies on the local system was one of the major concerns expressed by many respondents. In the 1988 survey, 85 of the respondents thought that the system could be improved if advice was given to the executive and legislature on the impact of policy innovation prior to its finalization. As the officials responsible for the implementation of policy changes, they would be in a good position to give considered opinions on policy innovation.

The discorrespondent nature of the system was commented on by many respondents from all the agencies who were aware of the inefficiencies and dysfunctions in a system that lacked cooperation and congruity, a system in which mutually impinging agencies regarded themselves as not answerable to each other and seemed unconcerned about the consequences for other agencies of autonomously determined policies and practices.

A police chief explained, "Agencies in a survival mode often make independent decisions that free resources in their agency, but have a negative spin-off in other parts of the system. Citizen demands for increased law enforcement result in an overload at court and in the jails, resulting in a revolving door syndrome ultimately leading to a disillusioned public" (p. 11).

Finally, the lack of coordination is accounted for by another sheriff as a consequence of resource inadequacies. "Every entity of the criminal justice system is attempting to keep their head above water with increased workloads, public expectations, understaffing, and funding cutbacks. There is little time for coordinating, cooperating, or communicating when you are up to your ass in alligators" (p. 11).

4

Penal Reform: Will It Be All Right on the Night?

From his grave in Highgate Cemetery in London, Karl Marx responds to questions from Martin Jacques, the editor of the journal *Marxism Today*. On the eve of the collapse of the communist bloc in Eastern Europe, Jacques constructs a fictional interview with Marx to get his response to the end of the socialist hegemony in Eastern Europe and the U.S.S.R. In this fictional interview printed in a London newspaper, Jacques asks Marx:

> *Jacques*: You wrote with extraordinary insight about capitalism, such that today many people who would never dream of calling themselves Marxists are influenced by your ideas. You wrote much about revolutions, particularly 1848 and the Paris Commune. And yet you wrote precious little about socialism. When the Bolsheviks took power they inherited little more than a blank piece of paper.
>
> *Marx*: I suppose we assumed that when the moment arrived it would be relatively clear what needed to be done. We

> were guilty, I guess, of a certain utopianism. *It would be all right on the night.* (*Financial Times*, 1990, p. B1)

Is it possible to avoid utopianism in the arena of penal reform? Whatever the level of change in our social institutions we might desire, the critics of utopianism warn us that we ignore at our peril the practical implications of reform.

The practical considerations require an evaluation of not only funding arrangements, but also the whole complicated array of social implications that follow a reform. How are you going to do it? Where will the personnel come from? What level of skills will they require? Is there administrative support and organizational spare capacity to bring about the planned reform? Is there public and professional receptiveness to the proposals? Public and professional resistance can undermine the good intentions of the best of planners. The use of focus groups will help to avoid some of the utopian pitfalls of the modern penal drama and increase the likelihood that innovations are not just another repeat episode in the ongoing "prisons-in-crisis" saga.

The collapse of the soviet empire is a timely reminder of the failure of utopianism—a utopianism driven by a vision of what was wrong with existing society. With social reform, be it on the scale of social revolution or penal reform, it is no longer sufficient to be motivated by a rejection of past or current social institutions, be they capitalism as a whole or prisons in particular. We are entitled to ask what is going to be put in their place, to know the details of these new arrangements of human affairs. One dimension of these new arrangements, vital in a democracy, is whether the public has confidence in the new idea. Public credibility is crucial to the success of reform, particularly in matters of sentencing and penal policy.

PENAL REFORM: WHEN THE PRACTICAL AND THE IDEOLOGICAL COINCIDE

Achieving sentencing or penal reform is not simply the application of a good idea. Reform of any social institution takes place within a cultural and structural context. Criminal justice and penal agencies are not autonomous; they operate within an administrative and social framework. Prisons cannot be successfully reformed in isolation from the criminal justice system, any more than they can be analyzed in isolation from the contextual realities of the system of which they are a part. Understanding how prisons are governed (cf. DiIulio) is not just a matter of the internal management of a large institution, but requires an understanding of how this institution interacts with other agencies in the criminal justice system, the legal and governmental structure, the socio-economic context, and the politico-cultural climate.

While internal and external pressures can build up for the reform of criminal justice agencies, the facility and incentive to do so in a systematic way is not encouraged or available. Malcolm Feeley wrote in *Court Reform on Trial*, "There is little incentive for those engaged in day-to-day administration of criminal courts to think about systemwide changes or, when they do, to pursue them vigorously. But when change comes, as we have seen, it is often initiated by 'dramatic events' and offered as a 'bold solution' that is promoted as a panacea. Such conditions do not give rise to serious thinking or realistic expectations" (1983, p. 192). Hence, Feeley sees reforms not as a result of imagination, planning and leadership, but as a short-term response to crisis and dislocation of the system.

It was the dislocation of the American Revolution that provided a practical problem to early penal administrators in England, leading to the Penitentiary Houses Act of 1779. Christopher Hibbert wrote, "Four years before, on 19th April 1775, the first shots of the American Revolution had been fired at Lexington and the Government had been obliged to face the fact that the transatlantic colonies could no longer be considered a convenient dumping-ground for unwanted men" (1978, p. 139).

There are parallels between penal reform and social change. Richard Tawney sees the catalyst for change coming from social dislocation. In his analysis of the social changes associated with the Reformation, he links the upheavals in the economic sphere resulting from emergent capitalism to the religious and cultural changes of the Reformation era. Tawney wrote in *Religion and the Rise of Capitalism*:

> It is not to underestimate the effect of the Reformation to say that the principal causes making the age a watershed from which new streams of social theory descend, lay in another region. Mankind does not reflect upon questions of economic or social organization until compelled to do so by some sharp pressure of some practical emergency. The 16th century was an age of social speculation for the same reason as the early 19th century — because it was an age of social dislocation. (1938, p. 76)

The need to solve a practical problem will invoke the need to scan the intellectual horizon to see what new ideas are available. One test will be the degree of receptiveness to the new idea by a number of constituencies, which include experts in the field, policy makers and policy implementers, and those who are the potential receivers of a service. Hence, the importance of having available a reform that has not been discredited previously. It is when the ideological and the practical coincide that reforms take place.

In California, there is some enthusiasm for a Community Corrections Act. For Californian officials, a Community Corrections Act will have implications for state and county budgets. Consequently, the negotiations over financial levels of subsidy, and the control over resource-related decisions, will be vital to state and county interests. Much effort will be invested in finding a politically and financially acceptable way to fund intermediate sanctions. Many policy makers in California seem to be overly concerned with the "bottom line" of funding. But as the last ten years have shown, spending great sums of money does not in itself result in greater public confidence in the criminal justice system.

The issue of public confidence about intermediate sanctions was one of the core questions raised in a series of focus group panels held in the summer of 1990 throughout California. The evidence from this empirical inquiry would suggest that public confidence, as interpreted by criminal justice officials, requires a composite form of sentence with multiple goals for intermediate offenses, and combining the aims of retribution, control, and rehabilitation. A degree of public reassurance is required to explain what will happen to those previously prison-bound offenders convicted of fraud, theft, non-domestic burglaries, and drug use, if they are to remain in the community.

Finding out more about the public mood is essential if a penal reform is to be successful. Hence, the interest on focus groups to gather information about the public's concern over matters of crime. Crucial for those starting with a denunciatory-retributive approach to punishment is an awareness of what will float with the public (i.e., a sensitivity to the community's confidence in sentencing proposals). Public confidence is one aspect of avoiding utopianism among penal reformers. Another is an awareness of the fiscal and economic interests at stake.

Funding is a crucial consideration that has to be addressed by the penal reformer. "In the past ten years, the Department of Corrections' operating budget has doubled and by 1991, the state will spend about one-tenth of its General Fund budget to maintain its correctional system if current correctional policies continue." So ran the preamble to Senate Bill 279 in 1987.

The criminal justice and penal budget in California has been the fastest growing sector of fiscal expenditure during the 1980s. Between 1982 and 1987, total dollar expenditures on criminal justice rose by 72 percent. From 1977, the budget for local jails has increased over 200 percent. From 1981 to 1987 the CDC's budget tripled. Despite this expenditure, all parts of the system experience capacity overload.

It is possible that the seventh richest economy in the world will continue to grow despite what happens elsewhere. But it will need to grow if it is to pay for the future demands on the penal system. The prison population of the CDC had expanded to reach 104,000 inmates by 1992. The latest demographic trends predict the total California population to grow in size by 500,000 every year until

1995. Labor costs are certain to rise, for in California the Correctional Peace Officers Union (CCPOA) is well organized.

The CCPOA has been noticeably generous with its campaign donations to politicians. Two legislators received $10,000 from them in 1988. Between $40,000 and $80,000 was spent to defeat a ballot initiative concerned with campaign reforms. "They are now the leading contributor to political campaigns among public-employee unions" according to James Richardson in the *Sacramento Bee*, (March 22, 1988) which continues, "This year, the guards have already given $316,374 to candidates and initiative campaigns." In 1988 their level of political contributions made them the fifth largest spender after the California Trial Lawyers Association, the Insurers Political Action Committee, the California Medical Association, and the corporation G. Tech. They are vying with professional associations and private corporations for political influence.

The 30,767 California Department of Corrections employees in 1992 have become another group with a vested interest in maintaining a policy of high-rate incarceration. With its political contacts and lobbying skills, it is bound to become another powerful, entrenched group that could restrict future policy options. It is hard to continue to think of prisons as simply a "religious" issue in political terms, a lot of "juice" is now at stake.

The criminal justice and penal system in California is not immune to the economic facts of life. By 1990 the state was running into fiscal difficulties. Even if all goes well with the economy, and labor costs do not become too burdensome, and the voters do not mind paying the tax bill, a future administration might well consider changing its policy priorities. By 1992 state funding was reaching a crisis level for the Department of Corrections as well as every other state agency. With less money available to operate the enlarged penal estate, the problems of overcrowding could create a situation for a statewide general condition of confinement lawsuit, adding to the tax bill of the state.

But one Californian's tax bill is another Californian's income. The rurally located small towns that suffer from localized economic recession used to pray for a railroad station or airport. Today in California the Chamber of Commerce representatives beat a path to the Department of Corrections to sell their town as the ideal location for a new prison. The Prison Construction and Operations Committee, a joint legislative committee chaired by Senator Robert Presley, holds public meetings to discuss the issue of prison planning and site location. Prison construction is the latest form of unofficial regional economic aid and results in "planning hearings" taking the form of a series of marketing talks from town representatives. In 1987 the two small towns of Avenal in King's County and Ione in Amador had population growths of 77 percent and 64 percent respectively. These fastest growing towns in the West had opened state prisons that year. They were the latest boom towns.

Most of the new prisons are being located in or near small and rural communities, in part because they want them and the larger urban areas do not. If these towns become economically dependent on the prison payroll, then this could be another rivet in the California penal system that locks it into a reliance on the use of high incarceration rates. When Director of the Department of Correction Ray Procunier tried to shut down Susanville prison in the early 1970s at a time of prison population decline, the populace of this small, rural, and remote community in Lassen County successfully lobbied, on the grounds of the town's dependence on the prison payroll, to overturn his decision.

Economic facts readily become the basis of political lobbying, of which there is no shortage in California or elsewhere when sentencing and penal policy is discussed.

The Politicization of Sentencing Reform

The concern with crime issues among the electorate and politicians is evident from the large number of legislative proposals that are introduced in the legislature each year. In 1987, 150 bills were introduced. Only one sought shorter prison terms. One quarter of all bills introduced annually concern criminal justice topics. From 1976 to 1986, of eighteen bills altering sentence lengths that were enacted, only two resulted in reduced time for offenders. Between 1980 and 1986, 187 bills that increased sentence lengths were passed by the legislature. This annual lottery makes for uncertainty and difficulty in planning for the future.

The process of democracy in states such as California requires that county and state law enforcement officers and judges be elected or re-elected. How are the political and ideological positions espoused in the campaign that led to the election of these public officers to be reconciled with the need for the law to be considered as a resource for all Californians and free from bias? The increasing cost of campaigning for elected judicial posts adds to the problem. The campaign to elect Malcolm Lucas to the California Supreme Court is estimated to have cost $11.4 million. An important distinction in politics, wrote Californian journalist Dan Walters in the *Sacramento Bee* newspaper "is whether one practices politics in order to make policy, or one uses policy to practice politics."

It is hard to disapprove of the politicization of crime in a democratic society; however, it has a number of potentially disturbing and distorting influences upon policy makers and practitioners alike for the following reasons:

1. A single incident such as a vicious crime or prison escape can be highlighted and given considerable media and public attention. This can require a disproportionate response in terms of time, money, and manpower to reassure the public and deal with the problem as a priority, whereas a more balanced view would have used resources on less salient but important aspects of the system.
2. There is a very selective focus on the crime problem. Media coverage of "newsworthy" stories, which focus on the more visible type of street crime or high profile cases in court and notorious criminals or inmates, presents an unrealistic picture to the public of the nature of the problems facing the criminal justice system as a whole.

3. Partisan political debate may polarize the issues, which can encourage unrealistic expectations among the public about the nature of the problem and the ability of governments to solve these problems. The subsequent failure to resolve the problem can result in the alienation of citizens from the political and criminal justice system.
4. Pressure on elected representatives and such officials as judges, sheriffs and district attorneys can result in short-term political goals having priority over such factors as justice for defendants or the protection of the community.

The problem for those responsible for the criminal justice system is that the politicization of crime issues is likely to encourage short-term and simplistic solutions, without necessarily providing information about the complexities or interdependencies in the system. To suggest that politics should be taken out of the public debate on crime policy would be unrealistic and unwise — unwise because in a democracy the protection of the citizens is the first duty of government, and the public is the best judge of that. However, some barrier and counterbalance to the politicization of crime policy formulation is required, either through the structure of political representation, such as through a parliamentary system of government, or through a policy-making body, such as a sentencing commission or council.

The public should have a say about sentencing policy; the issue is how to organize its input. A denunciatory-retributive approach requires that the public have confidence in the system of justice and feel that it reflects its values and concerns. But this does not require that the details of sentencing policy have to be dictated by plebiscite. There are three feasible strategies. First, over the long term, improve public awareness through a program of education and publicity. Second, in the shorter term introduce a filtering device, so as not to lead public opinion but to articulate it, clarify its ambiguities, and then represent it in a way that is consistent with the requirements of the criminal justice system. An improved system of public consultation is needed. Third, provide structural reforms such as a sentencing commission to act as a focus and a filter for new sentencing demands.

In a democracy, the long-term solution is to tackle the source of the problem by ensuring that the public is informed and aware of the complexities, costs, and multiple goals that are strived for in the criminal justice system. In the California survey (Davies, 1988a), the view that the public had little understanding of the problems of the agencies and that the system was too dependent on shifts in public opinion may explain the strong support for the proposal to conduct a survey of public knowledge of the system and promote better public understanding of the costs, conditions, and consequences of the system. Many decisions were dismissed as faddish, politically expedient and made to satisfy political interests, which often were determined by an uninformed public. Indicative of many was this statement by a presiding judge of a superior court. He blamed "The knee-jerk reaction of legislators to political pressure" for decisions made in Sacramento without "consideration of the impact they would have on local court or state facilities and for the lack of constructive measures on returning felons to the community to avoid recycling them back to prison" (p. 10).

The depoliticization of sentencing policy should also be regarded as a relative rather than an absolute issue. Complete depoliticization, would be desirable yet unlikely. However, the de-escalation of the political input into sentencing would have its advantages. To curtail the exploitation of crime issues in California politics would require a comprehensive reform of both the state's electoral and political system and the existing political culture. A more realistic approach might focus on the receiver, rather than the giver of the message. To this end, a long-term effort could be made to encourage greater awareness of the issues and look for a more sophisticated response from the public.

Efforts should be made to avoid some of the ideologically inspired rhetoric that has tended to polarize and politicize past debates over sentencing reform. The use of focus groups with panels made up of criminal justice officials would encourage both a consensus-building strategy and a system's perspective based on county-level criminal justice agencies. One institutional reform worthy of consideration, as it is thought to be capable of defusing some of the political tensions associated with sentencing policy, is the proposal to introduce a sentencing commission or council.

Sentencing Commission

Would a Sentencing Commission provide for greater regulation and depoliticization? In December 1982 Senator Presley introduced a bill into the California Legislature (Senate Bill 56), which proposed to establish a Sentencing Commission. It had the support of the Attorney General; the State Bar's Commission on Corrections; the California Correctional Peace Officers Association; the Citizens for Law and order; the California Parole, Probation and Correctional Association; and the American Civil Liberties Union. Opposing it were the Los Angeles County Sheriff, the California Public Defenders Association, and the California Attorneys for Criminal Justice. It passed in the Assembly with 55 votes in favor and none against and in the Senate with 24 in favor and 6 against. In September 1984 the governor vetoed the proposal, as he did with subsequent attempts by Senators Presley and Lockyer to introduce legislation to establish a sentencing commission.

The aim of the Presley bill was to establish a nineteen-member commission. It was to devise sentencing guidelines, which would include the following:

1. Recommend series of sentence ranges for all felonies to replace the determinate sentence (e.g., where determinate sentencing terms are two, three or four years, a range of two to six years would be recommended).
2. Recommend prosecuting standards in respect to charging offenses.

3. Recommend standards concerning consecutively or concurrently served sentences.
4. Emphasize imprisonment for the violent offender and alternatives for the non-violent offender.
5. If prison capacity were to be exceeded, to prepare a standard sentence list consistent with capacity.
6. Every two years recommend to the legislature revisions to the guidelines.
7. Advise the legislature of the consequences of sentence changes prepared by the legislature with respect to their impact on the capacity of the state correctional facilities.
8. Promote uniformity in sentencing.
9. Collect, analyze, and distribute quarterly information to trial judges and publish relevant information.
10. Study and review statutory sentences and the question of existing criminal penalties and report to the Governor and the legislature.

Sentencing commissions have been introduced in Florida, Minnesota, Pennsylvania, and Washington, as well as in the federal criminal courts. Michael Tonry commented, "Sentencing commissions are at work in several other jurisdictions and have tried but failed to produce guidelines . . . including South Carolina, New York and Maine. In other states, the organized judiciary has promulgated statewide sentencing guidelines" (1987, p. 6).

It was maintained in a report from Senator Presley's Office in support of the Presley Bill, that a sentencing commission would take some of the pressure off the legislature. The report states "The Legislature establishes sentences on a piecemeal, ad hoc basis, typically in response to public outcry over a particular incident. There is no systematic method for comparing the seriousness of different offenses or establishing relative sentence lengths" (Presley, 1983, p. 5).

The governor vetoed the bill. In a statement of September 1984 in defense of his decision he stated that the pattern of change in sentencing under the determinate sentencing laws was for the better and credited it with bringing about a reduction in major crime from 1981 to 1984. Second, he believed that the legislature should set prison sentence terms as it is directly responsible to the voters of California.

In California the pressure to introduce a sentencing commission has been resisted, but the issue of sentencing policy is recognized as central to the issue of penal overcrowding. In the United Kingdom similar awareness of the links between sentencing policy and penal overcrowding led to the proposal to introduce a sentencing council. This was rejected by the government. John Patten, a minister in the Home Office, in 1991 wrote in a letter to *The Times* of London, "Those who ponder sentencing councils must not ignore that which is already in place, potentially providing so much of what they want to see, but in a way that works with the grain of the criminal justice traditions in this country" (p. 32).

The Local Criminal Justice Culture

Going against the "grain of the criminal justice" culture is sometimes necessary to combat an entrenched inefficiency or injustice in the criminal justice system. However, to achieve reforms and to see policy changes successfully implemented, an awareness of the criminal justice culture is essential so as to avoid the utopianism of naive sentencing reform. Culture exists because it provides "a guide to living" both in terms of daily routines but also at the level of legitimating the everyday practical activities of people. This is as true of the criminal justice system as of any other area of life. Criminal justice cultures provide insight into how the practitioners define their world-taken-for-granted.

Michael Tonry, in his analysis of the effects of sentencing commissions on sentencing practice, argues that an understanding of the constraints imposed by the local legal and political culture will help to explain the different impact that sentencing commissions have had in the states that have introduced them. Tonry wrote:

> The Minnesota and Washington experiences suggest that the combination of sentencing commissions and presumptive guidelines is a viable approach for achieving consistent and coherent jurisdiction-wide sentencing policies. However, the experiences in Maine, New York, Pennsylvania, and South Carolina counsel that the sentencing commission approach won't necessarily succeed. Six jurisdictions are too few to support any but the most tentative generalizations about success and failure. Still, it is clear that most local legal and political cultures shape the environments in which the commissions work. Minnesota and Washington, for example, are both relatively homogeneous states with reform traditions. In neither state were criminal justice issues highly politicized. New York and Pennsylvania, by contrast, are heterogeneous states in which criminal justice issues are highly politicized and law-and-order sentiment is powerful. In some states, especially where trial judges are elected, judges may vigorously resist efforts to limit their discretion. Perhaps the only generalization that can be offered concerning political and legal culture is that the potential and the effectiveness of a sentencing commission will depend on how it addresses and accommodates constraints imposed by the local culture. (1987, p. 59)

For two hundred years the prison sentence has evolved as the primary form of punishment in terms of its saliency for public and judges throughout the United States. But society has changed considerably in that time from an industrial to an information society. Penal practice and ideology are not set in stone, but they are part of the modern state, with its large bureaucratic agencies — agencies that suffer from professional entrenchment, the disillusionment that nothing works, a crime problem that seems to inexorably worsen, and constitutional complexities that confound them. Criminal justice planning takes place in a climate of law and order, dictated by short-term electoral and economic cycles.

Into this complex scenario comes the penal reformer with an idea of what is wrong, say with the prison. The reformer needs to convince policy makers, practitioners and the public that change is needed. The attempts to avoid utopianism have concentrated on the questions "What works?" and "At what price?" A third necessary question is "Who accepts it?" Reforms will be more readily accepted if the reformer can show what will replace an apparently moribund institution, say the prison. But some dead bodies have come to life at the news of their demise. Public confidence has kept the prison alive, despite the continual cries that it is in crisis, and even though it does not fit easily with our collective self-image of a society approaching the twenty-first century. Prison is something of an embarrassment, but an embarrassment we seem prepared to live with because most people have confidence in it. And collective re-assurance is a major responsibility of the criminal justice system.

Collective re-assurance was my starting point in the analysis of punishment in this book. While sentencing innovations can be imposed, they potentially threaten to undermine public and professional confidence. Our response to crime is inextricably bound up with the question of credibility and confidence.

The system of consultation can and should be improved. It is naive to impose reforms that go against the grain of the local criminal justice culture. But it is also naive to think that criminal justice institutions, even if these are intrinsically conservative institutions, can remain the same. Better consultation will come about through regular feedback from public and professional opinion. One of the ways this can be done, and it has the virtue of being able to explain some of the complexities of the criminal justice system, is through the use of focus groups. Focus groups can act as just such a mechanism to provide information and feedback for both professionals who operate the system and the public as the "receivers" of the system.

GETTING IT RIGHT ON THE NIGHT: THE USE OF FOCUS GROUPS

What is a focus group? A focus group is made up of five to eight panelists who under the guidance of a moderator discuss in depth a narrowly specified topic. The discussion lasts between one to two hours but can be longer. The confidential responses of the panelists are recorded as data to help evaluate innovations. Focus groups have been used regularly in marketing, product development, and political campaigning to evaluate the potential uses of new products and new ideas. Focus groups are a qualitative research device, more akin to the in-depth interview. The success of the approach depends on the quality, rather than the quantity of the responses. The end product is a report based on a distillation of the comments of the panelists. These comments are not attributed to identifiable individuals or agencies.

The naturalness of the group discussion is a major advantage of the focus group as a qualitative research technique:

> Focus groups produce a very rich body of data expressed in the respondent's own words and context. There is a minimum of artificiality of response, unlike survey questionnaires, that ask for responses expressed on five-point rating scales or other constrained categories. Participants can qualify their responses or identify important contingencies associated with their answers. Thus responses have a certain ecological validity not found in traditional survey methods. (Stewart and Shamdasani, 1990, p. 12)

This approach is particularly appropriate for action research where the purpose is not just to understand a phenomenon, but to help formulate a change in policy, or to achieve the implementation of a policy. Focus groups were used in John Doble's study of citizens' views about punishment by the Public Agenda Foundation. Twelve focus groups were established, totaling 125 people. Each group met four times during 1986. Doble wrote that focus groups allow for "intense and directed discussions of public policy questions among small groups of men and women broadly representative of their fellow citizen. Focus groups are designed to probe issues more deeply than public opinion surveys can, allowing participants to explain their opinion in order to surface the assumptions that underlie those perspectives" (1987, p. 4).

The focus group is a technique used by researchers and policy analysts to gain insight into the perceptions, beliefs, experiences, views, and assumptions that underpin these subjective appreciations of the topic under inquiry. In this type of qualitative research, the "unit of analysis," to quote Robert Walker (1985), is made up of ideas and experiences.

As a technique of social investigation, focus groups have a number of advantages. They are cheaper and more flexible than other forms of data collection, and they provide data that has greater insight—that can be clarified in the more natural and relaxed setting of the group discussion. Below are the advantages identified by Stewart and Shamdasani in *Focus Groups: Theory and Practice*:

1. Focus groups provide data from a group of people much more quickly and at less cost than would be the case if each individual were interviewed separately. They can also be assembled on much shorter notice than would be required for a more systematic, and larger survey.
2. Focus groups allow the researcher to interact directly with the respondents. This provides opportunities for the clarification of responses, for follow-up questions, and for probing of responses. Respondents can qualify responses or give contingent answers to questions. In addition, it is possible for the researcher to observe nonverbal responses such as gestures, smiles, frowns and so forth, which may carry information that supplements (and, on occasion, even contradicts) the verbal response.

3. The open response format of the focus group provides an opportunity to obtain large and rich amounts of data in the respondent's own words. The researcher can obtain deeper levels of meaning, make important connections, and identify subtle nuances in expression and meaning.
4. Focus groups allow respondents to react to and build upon the responses of other group members. This synergistic effect of the group setting may result in the production of data or ideas that might not have been uncovered in individual interviews.
5. Focus groups are very flexible. They can be used to examine a idea range of topics with a variety of individuals and in a variety of settings.
6. Focus groups may be one of the few research tools available for obtaining data from children or from individuals who are not particularly literate.
7. The results of a focus group are easy to understand. Researchers and decision makers can readily understand the verbal responses of most respondents. This is not always the case with more sophisticated survey research that employs complex statistical analyses. (1990, p. 16)

The usefulness of any research technique is based on its appropriateness for certain types of inquiry. An understanding of the limitations of the focus group helps to determine whether it is inappropriate for certain types of inquiry. The limitations of the focus group approach are set out by Stewart and Shamdasani:

1. The small numbers of respondents that participate even in several different focus groups and the convenience nature of most focus group recruiting practices significantly limit generalizations to a larger population. Indeed, persons who are willing to travel to a locale to participate in a one- or two-hour group discussion may be quite

different from the population of interest, at least on some dimension, such as compliance or deference.

2. The interaction of respondents with one another and with the researcher has two undesirable effects. First, the responses from members of the groups are not independent of one another, which restricts the generalizability of results. Second, the results obtained in a focus group may be biased by a very dominant or opinionated member. More reserved group members may be hesitant to talk.
3. The "live" and immediate nature of the interaction may lead a researcher or decision maker to place greater faith in the findings than is actually warranted. There is a certain credibility attached to the opinion of live respondents that is often not present in statistical summaries.
4. The open-ended nature of the responses obtained in focus groups makes summarization and interpretation of results difficult.
5. The moderator may bias results by knowingly or unknowingly providing cues about what types of responses and answers are desirable. (1990, p. 17)

The live aspect of focus group interaction and the potential overreliance on this form of data seems to be the major danger of using the focus group, as is the temptation to use qualitative data to reach generalizable conclusions. The temptation and misuse of focus groups, according to Robert Merton (1987), "consists in taking merely plausible interpretations deriving from qualitative group interviews and treating them as though they had been shown to be reliably valid for gauging the distribution of responses" (p. 557).

Uses of Focus Groups for Policy Evaluation in the Criminal Justice System

Apart from the usefulness of focus groups as a means of social investigation, the methodology of focus groups can be employed to explore criminal justice policy innovations and the receptiveness of the public or the officials to policy proposals. The publication of the Blue Ribbon Commission's report provided the opportunity to invite criminal justice officials to discuss its recommendations in focus groups. In promoting discussion about the report and the future direction of reform of the criminal justice system in California, focus groups have a number of advantages.

First, there is exposure. A police chief who had not heard of the report was sent a copy, and all panelists were sent a summary. A judge at the end of a session volunteered the information that he had not read the report but would now, having been stimulated by the panel discussions. In the evaluation questionnaire sent afterward to all panelists, a second judge wrote, "I was unaware of the study and its conclusions before being asked to attend" (p. 3).

Second, there is saliency. Most of the panelists had heard of the report and read summaries of it prior to their invitation to participate in the focus group. However, the invitation to participate in a focused discussion on one aspect of the report encouraged a closer reading of the report by panelists. Also it might have encouraged some panelists to probe their colleagues' attitudes about the report and to generate discussion about its recommendations. After the meeting, a clearer picture of the implications of the report might have stimulated further discussion.

Third, there is clarity. This 132-page report covering many aspects of the criminal justice system in California was bound to have problems of interpretation.

Fourth, consultation and feedback is provided by responses from panelists to policy proposals. As Richard Krueger (1988) states, "Focus groups . . . are particularly effective in providing information about why people think or feel the way they do" (p. 14). By officials gathering to hear comments about policy innovation, problems can be avoided. Aspects of policy can be clarified, if necessary, and deemed appropriate or amended. Where officials are influential decision makers, their response is vital for the subsequent decision whether to progress with innovations. Their response will also influence the likelihood of the reform being successfully introduced and implemented. Whatever the reason and impetus for reform, if utopianism is to be avoided, it is important to understand the culture of those who are to interpret the reform and implement it.

There is a fifth potential advantage of using focus groups: they could be used to help build system-awareness among criminal justice officials. This is of particular relevance to the criminal justice system in California. The Blue Ribbon Commission's report highlights the need for a more systematic and comprehensive approach to the problems facing criminal justice and correctional agencies. In 1988 I conducted a survey with the cooperation of the California Attorney General and the University of California (Davies, 1989). The survey was sent to criminal justice officials in the counties (chief probation officers, chiefs of police, district attorneys, presiding judges, public defenders, and sheriffs). The 294 officials who replied to the survey identified many dysfunctional aspects of the current system. They gave examples that ranged from inadequate communications and cooperation to inter-agency rivalry and hostility.

In California, by inviting county and city officials responsible for the criminal justice agencies to take part in focus group discussions, it was possible to expose officials to the views and assumptions about crime and crime policy held by officials from other agencies. They were able to hear, in much more detail than is usual in the working committees in which they normally meet, the views of other agency heads. When they expressed an opinion, they did so in front of officials from other agencies.

I could have conducted interviews with seventy-three individuals. By choosing the focus group approach, I was able to hear views expressed by officials, not in the privacy of a one-on-one interview, but in the presence of officials from other criminal justice agencies. This may not have changed any views, but it allowed for the views from other parts of the system to be expressed and heard.

In California the criminal justice system has its roots in fifty-eight counties. If there was to be a better system of consultation, it seemed logical to build it upon these county units of government.

Consultation in some form or other is already operating in the counties through coordinating councils and county task forces. The panelists I sought for my focus group inquiry already met together to conduct business. However, they did not always have an opportunity to discuss policy developments from the viewpoint of the county criminal justice system. A panelist explained in my 1990 focus group inquiry that "the number of committees of short duration with a multiplicity of agenda topics allowed little time for in-depth exploration of new policies." Another participant expressed that it gave them the opportunity to reflect about what was happening and to meet other officials—not to haggle over budget items, but to discuss policy issues.

Furthermore, the view from a county perspective is not always effectively communicated to the state government other than in the form of representation by professional bodies, such as those acting on behalf of the district attorneys or the chief probation officers. These professional bodies have represented well the collective views of the district attorneys, chief probation officers, or sheriffs to the legislature and the governor. However, their success encouraged a perception of the system as a discrete number of isolated agencies rather than as an interdependent and cooperating system.

Members of each agency within the criminal justice system will perceive issues from their own perspective. Who is to provide wider vision? The focus group can be used proactively for policy innovation purposes by identifying not just the issues and concerns of officials, but potential leaders. The focus group was a sounding board to identify those who felt strongly about the issues and were prepared to lead in supporting or resisting change.

Could something be done that would simultaneously improve consultation between county officials and state policy makers, and also help build a stronger sense of system awareness at the local level? Focus groups would provide such a mechanism. The advantage of focus groups over other forms of public feedback on policy issues is that whereas the opinion poll is concerned with how often a view is expressed and the media with how "newsworthy" a view is expressed, the focus group is concerned with how cogently a view is expressed.

CALIFORNIA FOCUS GROUP STUDY

During the summer of 1990 a series of focus groups met across California. The purpose of this study was to assess the views of criminal justice officials about the recommendations of the inquiry into the state of the criminal justice and penal system conducted by the Blue Ribbon Commission. There were thirty-eight recommendations in the Blue Ribbon Commission's report. The commission recommended among many things the greater use of intermediate sanctions through the adoption of a Community Corrections Act, to create "a partnership" between state and local governments to significantly expand community sanctions for offenders.

A focus group approach was used because it would provide a system-perspective response to the commission's recommendations based on the exchange of views among the counties' criminal justice officials. The comments made in the focus group panels were analyzed to reveal the views of the officials to the Blue Ribbon Commission recommendation for an increase in the use of community-based intermediate sanctions.

The focus group inquiry in California was confined to those recommendations concerned with the expansion of punishment options. The commission's report explained the potential advantages of expanding the use of intermediate sanctions. "These sanctions would provide a continuum of choices for judges and parole authorities, as well as provide options which are both substantially more restrictive and structured than present-day routine probation" (Blue Ribbon Commission, 1990, p. 49). In effect, this became a discussion on the possible form, role, and acceptability of intermediate sanctions.

"I have made a list of studies done in the last 30 years which have contained recommendations similar to those of the Blue Ribbon Commission," wrote Jim Rasmussen, the head of the

Bureau of Criminal Statistics in Sacramento, in 1991. "There have been seven [in California]. We have taken the first step many times but never seem to be able to move on" (p. 1). If the idea of community-based intermediate sanctions was to progress beyond the stage of being just a good idea, the support of criminal justice officials would be required. Otherwise an intermediate sanctions policy would follow the route of other utopian developments. To discover the thoughts about intermediate sanctions among criminal justice officials, a focus group inquiry was undertaken.

Eleven focus groups met in nine counties between May and August 1990. The following six local officials were invited to attend as panelists in each county: chief probation officer, district attorney, presiding judge of the superior court, presiding judge of the municipal court, public defender, and sheriff.

In addition, where appropriate, chiefs of police were invited and the head of the local department of corrections. In two counties, members of the board of supervisors were invited, and in three counties, analysts from the county executive's office. In one county, the director of the pretrial services unit was invited; in another, the county drug program administrator. In two counties, court administrative officers were sent invitations but did not attend.

Seventy-three panelists attended the eleven groups. Typical attendance was six or seven panelists, with a range of four to nine panelists. In one county, three focus groups were held with different panelist compositions: county set (a panelist from each agency); judges only; and lawyers only—judges, public defender, prosecutor, and court administrators.

Each panelist was sent an initial letter of invitation with a brochure explaining the background of the project. They were asked to indicate their willingness to participate. Substitution was encouraged when a person could not attend or thought that there was a more appropriate person in the agency. Several presiding judges of the superior court suggested that the judge in charge of the criminal calendar would be more appropriate. Once a list of potential panelists was established, a summary of the Blue Ribbon Commission's report was sent to each person, along with the list of questions to be discussed. These questions were intended to be a guide to discussions rather than an agenda to be rigidly followed.

Of the nine counties visited, six were counties with populations over 500,000: Contra Costa, Los Angeles, Riverside, Sacramento, San Francisco, and Santa Clara. The other three were medium-sized counties with populations between 100,000 and 500,000: Napa, Solano, and Sonoma. The 1989 total population of the nine counties visited was 14,569,800. This represented 50 percent of California's population of 29,063,000.

Content Analysis

Recordings were made at each of the sessions. A reading and rereading of the transcript of these meetings was followed by a content analysis and a summary report. The summary is a synthesis of the comments as expressed and recorded in the transcripts of the panel discussions. But an edited summary is bound to be selective and dependent upon the categories used in the content analysis. A summary report should explicitly distinguish between those categories used in the content analysis that derive internally and are source related (i.e., are categories that have emerged from the discussions) and those that are externally generated by policy or theoretical concerns.

My summary was knowingly influenced by three considerations. My first criteria was source related and internal to the data, and derived from the transcript. I attempted to provide an accurate account of the nature and substance of the discussions that took place. It involved asking the question, "Would the majority of participants regard the summary as a reasonable account?" Second was an external criteria of policy-related relevance. Would the majority of participants regard this summary as acceptable as a framework for policy discussions in the future, and would it relate to the current policy initiatives within the criminal justice system in California as described in the Blue Ribbon Commission's report? The third criteria for selecting material for the summary report was context related.

The political and economic context, and not-so-hidden agenda affecting the move toward a partnership between state and local government, and a greater use of state-subsidized, community-based intermediate sanctions, involved the following political and resource issues: (1) The counties are short of funds and since January 1991 so is the State of California; (2) the counties in California are highly suspicious of agreements involving state funding, and they fear "bait and switch" consequences that will result in state prisoners being dumped on the counties at the counties' expense; (3) finding non-controversial locations to build correctional facilities in urban areas has been a problem for the state; (4) there is little political leadership available in this field of public policy and considerable concern among elected representatives and officials that the public might construe moves toward community corrections as being soft on criminals; and (5) concern over the level of crime, as the recorded crime level, and the public's anxiety about crime remains high.

How did the seventy-three panelists feel about their participation in the focus group discussions? Some comments were made during the discussions. One district attorney, who identified himself as a doubting Thomas, made clear his suspicion that most research is conducted to prove the points already held by the researcher. Another offered the view that he thought they were dealing with a used car salesman. However, most casual comments offered during the focus groups indicated a favorable response to the opportunity to have time to discuss a single policy issue in depth with colleagues from other agencies, colleagues who they would normally meet with to deal with multi-item agendas concerned with operational problems or budgetary issues. One offered the view that the meeting was an opportunity to let off steam.

In an evaluation questionnaire sent to panelists after the meeting, the overwhelming majority indicated that they thought it was a useful experience and would attend another focus group, if the topic was of interest to them. A questionnaire was sent to all of the seventy-three panelists who took part in the focus group panels. Replies were received from sixty-six (90 percent). The questionnaire sought information about the convenience of the location, the duration of the session, the number of sessions, ways of improving the conduct of the meeting, the size of the group, and the suitability of the introductory, stimulus, and support material. We also asked whether they would attend another panel. The questionnaire asked, "Given an appropriate topic of interest to you and your agency, would you attend a future meeting, or recommend a colleague to do so?" Out of the sixty-six who responded, fifty-nine indicated yes, two no, and five did not respond to this question.

Another question in the evaluation survey asked, "Did you find the focus group a useful way of expressing your views?" Of the sixty-six panelists who responded to the survey, forty-eight agreed that it was useful, four did not find it useful, and fourteen made other comments or did not comment. The panelists were asked to explain their comments on whether or not the focus group was a useful way to express their views. Many took this as an opportunity to continue the debate and made further points about the substantive topic. Some commented on the process. A favorable view was expressed by a judge, who wrote, "Rarely is there any type of forum to explore these issues with other agencies that are in a position to influence change." A sheriff wrote, "There are limited opportunities available for expressing views that have statewide implications." A public defender wrote, "All who were there have direct knowledge of the problems and work with it everyday, so we could speak with first hand information and share our own concerns with each other." A superior court judge wrote, "There was a good interplay of ideas."

Assessing the usefulness of a focus group approach to policy development is still open to inquiry. What this study showed is that they could be set up; key actors did attend; and subsequent interactive discussions generated views that should help clarify issues with respect to the development of community corrections. In providing feedback for legislators and in helping to build a consensus of opinion for reform, a focus group approach seems to have some value.

Reforms, be they radical or evolutionary, are more likely to have an instrumental, as distinct from a symbolic, impact if they are built upon an awareness of the perceptions and experiences of those who are to translate them into action. A negative response by practitioners does not prevent reform. One possible conclusion that might result from negative feedback from practitioners is that a different or newly formed agency will have to be responsible for implementing any new scheme. An example from the United Kingdom shows the importance of assessing professional group confidence in proposals for penal reform. The legislation to provide for stiffer community-based sentences was enacted in 1991. However, those sections of the Criminal Justice Act that allow for electronic monitoring and home curfew will not succeed if its implementation is left to the probation service, whose members have voiced antipathy toward these reforms. That is to say that an understanding of the culture of criminal justice officials, and its constituent parts, is an essential prerequisite if utopianism is to be avoided by those who seek to bring about sentencing and penal reforms.

Finally, public confidence in the criminal justice system is important if not essential for a democratic society. From a denunciatory-retributive perspective, it is vital because of the role of punishment in the identification of the values that define a community and the people in it. One aspect of sentencing reform that should always be considered, along with other critical considerations such as its effectiveness, costs, fairness, and administrative implications, is the public's perception of the reform. Assessing the public's response is a sophisticated issue in a pluralistic society. It requires greater sensitivity than is possible by an exclusive reliance on opinion surveys. Hence, the need for focus groups to supplement existing means of community feedback about the plausibility of sentencing reforms.

5

What Role for Intermediate Sanctions?

What is the role for intermediate sanctions, given a perspective in which the multiple goals of punishment are recognized, but a synthesis of denunciation and retribution defines the primary purpose and sets the framework of the criminal justice system? Before I discuss the implications of this perspective for intermediate sanctions, I would like to make three points to put the issue into context.

First, community sanctions are not new and should not be presented as such. Intermediate sanctions, defined as a sentencing option between prison and probation, have been available for some time. The Los Angeles Municipal Court Judges' Association describes community service as the most popular alternative to jail used by the twenty-four municipal courts in Los Angeles County. In the year 1988–1989, 66,000 convicted offenders were ordered to perform 6 million hours of community service, a 47 percent increase from the previous year. The most widely used sentencing option for adult felony convictions is probation with jail. This is used in 60 percent of all adult felony dispositions in the superior courts.

Second, in the past intermediate sanctions have been presented as alternatives to incarceration. This was a mistake. The use of community services, fines, intensive supervision, home confinement, conditions attached to probation, and routine reporting have existed, but they are not alternatives to imprisonment. They are choices available to sentencers when they seek something other than incarceration, which should be clearly reserved for the more serious offenses and offenders. The introduction of this "secondary" punishment is not an attempt to replace the primary form, but to complement it.

The failure of prisons to rehabilitate or deter offenders sent to them gives a potential rationale for making less use of imprisonment but does not define a role for intermediate sanctions. For those whose crime does not require a prison sentence, we should have sentencing options that do not make their propensity to commit crime any greater in the future. Imprisonment is likely to make matters worse in terms of future behavior, therefore, when appropriate individual offenders are identified, they should be given a form of punishment other than incarceration. In the current debate this assumes a form of punishment served in the community. The irony is that it is the influences of the community, be they peer pressure, home environment, economic factors or mere opportunity, that are believed to cause crime. Thus, the problem is that while prison breeds criminality, so does the community.

The third point is the idea that the greater use of intermediate sanctions will reduce the demand for prison space and cost less than incarceration. However, the savings might in some cases be illusory, given that marginal costs of imprisonment will not effect savings until staff are laid off or prisons closed. Furthermore, the cost of effective forms of intermediate sanctions, through the need for staff follow-up, and the cost of offering multidimensional programs to offenders will be costly. However, as with alternatives to custody, it would be better to define a purpose for intermediate sanctions, rather than maintain merely that they are cheaper. So what purpose can intermediate sanctions have?

THE GOALS OF INTERMEDIATE SANCTIONS

Policy documents should offer specific objectives for intermediate sanctions, which must be clearly explained if the public is to have confidence that those offenders, who by their actions are perceived as a threat to the community, should be allowed to continue to live in the community.

Intermediate sanctions can fulfill a number of purposes, including the administrative goal of reducing the institutional population, although a more convincing rationale for intermediate sanctions is provided by a mixture of surveillance, retribution, and rehabilitation.

Retribution is required to assure that this category of offender is held accountable in terms of the principle of just deserts. Punishment must be distinct for these intermediate categories of offenses, from token sanctions for the more trivial offenses to imprisonment for the most serious offenses. Control and surveillance are required to provide some degree of public assurance that these previously prison-bound offenders convicted of fraud, theft, non-domestic burglaries and drug use will not continue their criminal behavior if left in the community.

A criminal justice system should attempt to balance the multiple purposes of sentencing. However, a denunciatory-retributive perspective will point out that if you only stress the importance of costs or rehabilitation, then you are likely to lose public confidence in the criminal justice system as a whole.

The Blue Ribbon Commission sees intermediate sanctions as fulfilling more than one penological role and talks of "punitive responses," "rigorous supervision" and "meaningful programming":

> Collectively, the proposed intermediate sanctions or punishment options represent a continuum of graduated sanctions, as an expansion of existing punitive responses that provide for (1) rigorous offender supervision in community settings; (2) renewed emphasis on programming and structured activity, both in custody and in community supervision, and (3)

> meaningful programming for offenders based on individualized need and the risk factors associated with continued criminal behavior and return to custody. (p. 49)

Rehabilitation with this category of adult offenders should be a goal of community-based intermediate sanctions. Rehabilitative efforts, previously the system's goal, should be concentrated on this category of offender. Rehabilitation will not be cost-effective or acceptable, either with lesser offenders, for there are too many, or with the most serious offenders, for it is too late once they are destined for prison, as prisons are now recognized as rehabilitatively counterproductive. Correctional efforts within the criminal justice system should be directed at achieving, where appropriate, lifestyle interventions with offenders convicted of intermediate level offenses. To achieve this multipurpose approach to community corrections, most criminal justice officials recognize the need for a more systematic and comprehensive approach to both sentencing policy and correctional practice.

Rehabilitation should not be the paramount goal of intermediate sanctions. Many offenders are already given a community sentence with the express goal of rehabilitation, but for lesser offenses. However, intermediate sanctions are to be used with offenders who have committed more serious offenses that would typically have led to imprisonment. From a denunciatory-retributive perspective, it is necessary to recognize that the offenders are being punished for the offense committed; second, they will be under control and supervision while in the community under sentence; and third, rehabilitative efforts will take place within the framework established by retributive and surveillance concerns. Rehabilitation, as part of the logic of intermediate sanctions, should not have priority over the other two goals of surveillance and punishment.

Surveillance

Surveillance, greater than is usually associated with routine probation, must be provided when dealing with a population of more serious and persistent offenders. The role of monitoring becomes vital in assuring the public that they are being protected. In recent years, more effective means of surveillance in community settings have been developed (e.g., 24-hour reporting systems, electronically monitored home confinement, intensive supervision).

The California Blue Ribbon Committee's report refers to the potential use of intermediate sanctions for offenders sentenced to short terms in the state prison. Some short-term inmates could avoid imprisonment. "If there were reasonable and safe intermediate sanctions, including community detention, to deal with these populations, the benefits to public safety through brief commitments to prison becomes increasingly questionable" (p. 41–42).

Without the degree of incapacitation or surveillance provided by a period of incarceration, it is possible to regard the surveillance of an offender's movements through regular contacts or electronic monitoring as an aspect of public protection. Community surveillance works through offender self-discipline, motivated by the anticipation of inspection. What Foucault (1977) regards as a menacing threat to individual liberty can be regarded as a limited attempt to encourage law-conforming behavior by offenders.

Electronic monitoring has proven to be popular across the United States. The estimated daily population in the United States of offenders on electronic monitoring has risen from 95 in 1986, to 826 by 1987, to 2,277 by 1988 and 6,490 by 1989. This represents a rapid escalation of use, although these numbers are thought to be an underestimate by Marc Renzema and David Skelton, the principal researchers who conducted the monitoring exercise for the National Institute of Justice (1990).

Net-widening is a worry for some critics of the introduction of intermediate sanctions, especially sanctions that are more demanding than routine probation. Stan Cohen (1985) suggests that more deviants will be processed, with enhanced levels of intervention and surveillance. And new sanctions will supplement rather than replace the original set of control mechanisms—that is, a wider, denser and different set of nets. Andrew Scull's decarceration message is rewritten. Maeve McMahon (1990) describes it thus (McMahon, 1990). "Scull modified his story of decarceration to that where alternatives were earlier seen by him as representing neglect of deviants, they were later seen as involving more control of offenders" (p. 123).

McMahon's analysis astutely points out that "net-widening in terms of correctional population counts is by definition a feature of alternatives to imprisonment" (p. 138). This point is readily appreciated when it is realized that an average prison sentence of 31 days in the United Kingdom is likely to be replaced by a probation order lasting 365 days. The total number of offenders therefore under the penal umbrella of the "punitive city" at any one time is bound to appear to rise even though the total population dealt with by the courts is the same.

In the United Kingdom, the view of one professional interest group is that "over-stringent requirements on offenders" involving punitive non-custodial penalties would, as the chairman of the National Association of Probation Officers, John Roberts told the annual conference in 1990, lead to "a big increase in the number of offenders jailed for failing to observe the terms of probation or community service sentences" (p. 3). He went on to blame courts' excessive use of imprisonment as the source of the problem and predicted that the present strategy to introduce tougher community-based sanctions would backfire. Consider the logic of this reductionist and net-widening type of argument. It reduces issues of criminal justice to policies that are constrained by the limitations of offenders. This is an important consideration but surely not the only one, especially when we are not talking about fine defaulters but burglars and persistent thieves who would otherwise be heading for a prison sentence.

The target population for intermediate sanctions has been identified by most theorists and policy documents as prison-bound offenders. The fear of the net-wideners, with respect to the use of intermediate sanctions, is that those offenders previously given a discharge, a fine, or routine probation will now be swept up, not only in a wider net, but in a more demanding net that imposes more controls and sanctions on the offender. This is likely and even, in cases, desirable. Only if we believed that the past "binary" system was working perfectly, would there be no doubts that all offenders got what they deserved, that there were no inconsistent sentences, no "lucky" offenders, or, most likely, no lack of appropriate sanctions because of inadequate resources or overcrowded facilities.

"From our research, we realized that many promising community-based correctional innovations, specifically alternative sentencing programs, failed to live up to their potential," wrote John Larivee (1990) in an article on Day Reporting Centers. "We found," he continued, "that instead of serving their intended population—otherwise incarcerated offenders—they often attracted offenders who would have received probation" (p. 87). This interpretation of an intermediate sanction's "failing" could be viewed as an incentive for a more refined tariff of sentences, whether for retributive, surveillance or rehabilitative purposes. Perhaps alternative sentencing programs are "living up to their potential" by offering a greater choice to sentencers. Obviously, the sentencers thought so.

Punishment

The comment of the Blue Ribbon Commission that imprisonment is not the only form of punishment suggests another role for intermediate sanctions, which is particularly important from a denunciatory-retributive perspective. A refinement of the tariffs of punishments is possible. Somewhere between "getting off" and "doing time" there is a gap. This gap in the "binary system" of sentencing provides a potential role for intermediate sanctions to be regarded as intermediate punishment. Retribution is not a simple theory of just "lock'em up." It requires, through the principle of proportionality, for the level of seriousness of the punishment to relate to the level of the seriousness of the offense.

The authors of the Blue Ribbon Commission *Report on Inmate Population Management* believed that "in sentencing decisions judges lack sufficient intermediate sanctions between routine probation and incarceration." A district attorney commented:

> We have to expand the punishment options, and get the public to understand this is not letting somebody off from doing his time. What we are doing is providing a system of more accountability and more control and the only difference is now we are dealing with some of these people locally as opposed to spending a lot of money sending them to prison through a revolving door. (Davies, 1991a, p. 8)

In California, the 1976 Uniform and Determinate Sentencing Law established the importance of proportionality with respect to the seriousness of the offense as being a guiding principle of sentencing policy. The proportionality principle, in the case of community sanctions, requires a range of penalties with varying degrees of restriction on the offender's liberty.

From the offenders' perceptions of punishment, some forms of intermediate sanctions (e.g., home curfew and electronic surveillance) are seen as undesirable and more punitive than jail and sometimes prison. This view of the hardships of community-based sanctions should be built on, to provide a punishment rationale for intermediate sanctions—a rationale that could be used to reassure the public. Public confidence in community corrections is a key to the success of intermediate sanctions.

Unringing the Bell of Rehabilitation

A judge in California, commenting on the shift in mood about punishment, suggested that a "swing of the pendulum" is unlikely to "turn back the clock" when it comes to the public's attitude toward rehabilitation:

> The public and legislature during the last decade indicated clearly that they want greater emphasis on public protection and punishment. We have had a flood of tough laws mandating minimum sentences; emphasizing punishment over rehabilitation; and now I think that the pendulum is starting to

> swing back the other way. I don't know whether we are ever going to completely un-ring that bell. (Davies, 1991a, p. 7)

However, as Cullen et al. (1988) wrote, "There is a duality to the public's sanctioning ideology. . . . While citizens clearly want offenders punished, they continue to believe that offenders should be rehabilitated" (p. 305). The public perception that imprisonment means that offenders are sent away for a long period of time is misleading. In California, 40,000 inmates will return to the community in less than six months, and they return probably worse than when they went to prison.

The Blue Ribbon Report regards rehabilitation as desirable, even though the word is only used twice in the report. However, the report makes frequent reference to changing offenders' behavior, of the need to provide for offender programs, and of holding offenders accountable for their actions. Thus there is still a commitment to rehabilitation, but not one based on the pre-1960s assumption of determinism.

The commission recommended the introduction of a Community Corrections Act that would expand the range of intermediate sanctions to meet two distinctive goals. "Such sanctions should function as punishment, as well as provide the offender with the opportunity through programs, training and work to change their criminal behavior" (p. 114).

The authors of the Blue Ribbon Commission report argue that public protection would be enhanced if offenders' behavior could be modified. Offenders kept in the community "retain their ties to family, jobs, and the community, thereby ultimately enhancing the likelihood of a successful reintegration into the community" (p. 119). But this would not be easy, as most panelists recognized. The community was also a source of criminality, and a list of community-based causes of crime was identified, which includes unemployment, peer pressure, drug subculture, family and housing problems.

Intermediate sanctions are used in the Blue Ribbon Report to refer not just to sentencing options, but also as an option available to the Department of Corrections for use at the pre-parole stage. "Prior to release on parole the inmate should be encouraged to develop a personal parole plan and participate in an intensive pre-release program" (p. 89). They recommended that the last 120 days of each offender's institutional stay could be an opportunity to use intermediate sanctions to facilitate re-entry and reintegration into the community.

The commission does not regard these limited rehabilitative aspirations as constituting a soft option. In the case of the increasing numbers of parolees returned because of drug violations, it recognized the need for a demanding and if necessary escalating regime, "A concentrated, hard hitting and continuously escalating series of intermediate sanctions and prison programs could serve to intervene with this behavior" (p. 44).

Proponents for and against the idea of adopting a rehabilitative role for intermediate sanctions agreed that the success rate was bound to be low. A chief of police in Los Angeles said: "I can remember the same failure rate with probation that you have today, and the same failure rate with parole that you have today. It hasn't changed one bit. You keep doing it. We have a failure rate that private industry would look at and say we have to go out of business because with that failure rate, we can't make a buck" (Davies, 1991, p. 10).

In reply, a Los Angeles public defender commented, "They don't have the Rhodes scholars on probation or parole. It is a success if 5% of them make it" (Davies, 1991, p. 10).

A COCKTAIL OF A SENTENCE: MAKING INTERMEDIATE SANCTIONS PALATABLE

To fill the void between prison and probation, intermediate sanctions have to provide:

- a graduated continuum of restrictions on liberty, to meet retributive and denunciatory demands.

- a flexible method of monitoring which can be enhanced or reduced depending on an offender's progress, to satisfy surveillance requirements.
- a range of multiple services and programs.

To achieve these goals, intermediate sanctions will have to be adequately funded, and their goals must be understood and well organized. The design of a successful cocktail to suit individual customers requires that the following qualities are recognized as vital ingredients of a community-based system of punishment:

- comprehensiveness
- multi-facetedness and flexibility
- multiple services and programs
- continuity of monitoring

Comprehensiveness

Comprehensiveness and a systematic approach are the key qualities required if intermediate sanctions are to succeed as a multipurpose form of punishment.

First, for the rehabilitative element, there must be a comprehensive and wide range of service providers, whose tasks are coordinated so that offenders with multiple problems can be helped in a way that is likely to achieve life-style changes. More flexibility and less bureaucratic compartmentalization are required if the multilevel and multiple causes of crime are to be tackled. This cannot be done in a piecemeal way. A judge explains why:

> One of the reasons we have so much recidivism in these young offenders is that they have no family, never gone to school, they are uneducated, have no job skills, they can't fill out an application, and they have never learned to get up in the morning. If they do get the job, they get fired because they don't report or get there on time. You have got to recognize

> you are not only dealing with the offender. You can take offenders and put them out in the desert and with supervision and training you could do a lot with those people. But if you return them to the communities where the houses are dilapidated and rundown with no electricity and the bathrooms don't work, then time after time these defendants will tell me "there is nothing I can do to help myself, judge." (Davies, 1990, p. 15)

Second, there are discontinuities in authority in relationship to the offender in the system. Whatever the reason, be they surveillance or rehabilitative goals, the bureaucratically and professionally dysfunctional behavior of law enforcement, courts and correctional agencies must be remedied so that a more comprehensive, cooperative and systematic approach is achieved in the criminal justice process. One characteristic of the current system in California, identified by the officials who took part in the focus groups, was a lack of continuity in handling offenders. The offender is processed through the many agencies in the system, with new files being produced by each agency. The offender is subjected to interviews with each one. One official, contrasting the process of the system with the outcome, suggested that the most punitive element of the criminal justice system for many arrestees was the interviewing and re-interviewing that takes place. The offender is bounced around among the police, sheriff, courts, jail, probation, prison, and parole. In contrast, the response to the offender should be integrated. A case-management approach based on the assessment of risk and needs, and depending on whether the continuity of authority is required for surveillance or rehabilitative purposes, should be adopted.

Third, a more comprehensive sentencing approach is needed. Judges should have sentencing options available that are properly regarded as severe without requiring imprisonment. This, of course, would all be made easier if the sentencing system were made more systematic by a more comprehensive set of guidelines, generated by a sentencing council or commission whose responsibility was to establish sentencing principles and policies, and maintain a monitoring role over the use of sanctions.

A comprehensive approach to sentencing would be essential given the likelihood of multidimensional intermediate sanctions, resulting in a compound sentence, with a cocktail of elements to achieve rehabilitation, restitution, retribution, and surveillance. The sentencer should have clear guidance as to how the ingredients could be mixed together so as not to overburden the offender, while reassuring the community in terms of public safety and provide for broad equality and commensurability between equally serious offenses. It is important to keep the decision on individual sentences within the confines of strictly agreed upon guidelines, given the potential mix of community service, compensation schemes, rehabilitative programming, home confinement, electronic monitoring, day reporting, and intensive supervision. Without guidelines, there is considerable potential for distortion, as the new compound sentences become part of the process of sentence negotiations, and professional manipulation (i.e., as defense counsels and probation officers seek a "better deal for their clients").

A fourth sense of comprehensiveness concerns the general justifying aim of the institutions of the criminal justice system. If this was clearly spelled out in denunciatory-retributive terms, the rationale of rehabilitation could play a part, within the context of very severe punishment for the worst offenses and token sanctions for the minor offenses. Correctionalism could find its niche by focusing on the mid-range offender.

A fifth reason for adopting a more comprehensive approach is that the criminal justice system is interdependent, as I have illustrated in chapter 2. Whatever the overarching mission of the criminal justice system, it will be more effectively achieved if there is coordination of resources and efforts by the various agencies that constitute the system. Intermediate sanctions will have a greater chance of making an impact on the crime problem if all the agencies, from law-making to corrections, act together.

Multifacetedness and Flexibility

Not only should intermediate sanctions be multipurposed; they should allow for multiple elements (i.e., community work, curfews, day reporting, electronic monitoring, fines, intensive probation supervision, mediation, programming, reparation, restitution, and work). But flexibility of form should not result in ambiguity of purpose at the time of sentence. Should it rehabilitate the offender, all well and good; if it does not, nothing is lost as the purpose of surveillance and punishment has been served. Most officials in the focus group sessions regarded work-oriented activities as desirable for they simultaneously could be considered as punishment, would require some degree of surveillance and might have rehabilitative properties.

Restitution could be part of the package of community-based intermediate sanctions. Restitution involves mediation and reparation. Mediation schemes require the intervention of a third party to resolve a conflict by coming to some form of settlement. Reparation involves the offender's paying back the victim for some of the harm caused by the commission of an offense. The issue for theorists of intermediate sanctions is not whether mediation and reparation schemes should exist, but whether they should form part of the process of prosecution and sentencing, and whether participation in such schemes should influence prosecution and sentencing decisions.

Restitution schemes should be done for their own sake to prevent these schemes getting embroiled in sentence bargaining. To avoid this, restitution could be offered as an entirely voluntary scheme between offender and victim, with no subsequent impact on sentencing decisions. Restitution, as an aspect of sentencing, might satisfy the private emotional needs of some victims, but not others, resulting in problems of sentencing equity when unwilling victims refused to cooperate. But a more important consideration is that sentencing policy is not a private matter between victim and offender. The public is entitled to input into sentencing decisions at the policy level. If restitution is to be part of the community-based sanctions available to the courts, then comprehensive guidelines and monitoring are essential to ensure consistency and uniformity in sentencing practice.

The California report refers to the need to use combinations of existing community sanctions to achieve intermediate sanction. The authors of the Blue Ribbon Commission report concluded that "incarceration is but one of an extensive set of potential sanctions which could be imposed upon offenders. When one considers that these options can be used alone or in combination, then the potential number of options becomes extensive" (p. 47). The report spells out those main options:

> California now principally employs punishment options or sanctions that represent two extremes in terms of both supervision and punitive value. Incarceration is clearly the most punitive and entails the maximum level of supervision and control. In contrast, probation supervision in California today is often little more than unsupervised community release and monitoring for re-arrest because the underfunding of probation frequently results in unmanageable caseload sizes. (Blue Ribbon Commission, p. 48)

The report identifies the following punishment options that provide on their own, or in combination, for a continuum of graduated intermediate sanctions:

electronic surveillance

house arrest

intensive probation and parole supervision

specialized parole and probation caseloads

work furlough

community service victim restitution centers and programs

community detention options

residential and non-residential substance abuse treatment programs

other community-based programs in both the private and public sectors
(Blue Ribbon Commission, p. 49)

Flexibility of form could be an element of intermediate sanctions at both the sentencing stage and in the subsequent period of correctional monitoring. First, this should permit sentencers, within guidelines based on offense and offender characteristics, to impose composite sanctions depending on a judgment of the risks and needs of the offender. Second, this type of sentence should have built-in, phased decreases and increases in surveillance, depending on the offender's progress, as judged by correctional agents.

Flexibility was considered to be important during the correctional period so that phased decreases in surveillance would be possible, depending on the offender's progress. But if the offender does not respond to the programs offered, then there should be the flexibility in the system to remove the offender from a particular community-based program.

Multiple Services and Programs

With rehabilitation as an aim of intermediate sanctions, it is necessary to understand the causal influences upon criminal action. These causes are many and complex. Hence, a method for the diagnosis of offender needs is required, as well as a wide range of services and programs to respond to those needs. If crime has its roots in the community, as maintained by the Blue Ribbon Commission, then the range of causally related factors is considerable. Subsequent programs could at a minimum require multiple programs and services geared to each inmate after a screening process had been completed. An initial list of services would include family counseling, work training, employment opportunities bureau, mental health services, literacy and educational courses, housing, welfare, social skill training, drug abuse programs, and drug use monitoring.

The question "what works?" in terms of behavior modification strategies stimulated discussion in the focus groups held in California in 1990 as to the causes of crime. The dilemma of whether crime should be regarded as an issue of individual responsibility and accountability or has its roots in social conditions was never resolved, but it underpinned many of the comments made by the panelists. It is the unresolved intellectual issue that informs and frustrates crime prevention efforts.

To provide a comprehensive range of multiple services would be costly and require the recognition and tolerance of a relatively low success rate. The following are the major problems that need to be treated:

alcohol
drugs
education
employment
family
housing
immaturity
inadequate social skills
influence of subcultural life-styles
irresponsibility
illiteracy
mental illness
underclass life opportunities

Are community correctional centers or probation/parole hostels required as part of the range of facilities to achieve intermediate sanction? Is there a need for a new style of residential institution, similar to a low security jail with programs? The idea of less secure, dormitory style institutions was recommended by the Blue Ribbon Commission. The commission members recognized that many offenders sent to custody are not a major security problem and do not require the costly custodial conditions required for prison and jail. One judge was not impressed with the novelty of the community correctional center. He commented, "It's the old half-way house concept with different whistles and bells on it" (Davies, 1991, p. 12).

In California local officials were not very sympathetic to the idea of a joint state-local community correctional center. A potential model of such a facility was provided by California Senate Bill 2000 to allow for substance abuse community correctional centers. These would be built with state funds and operated on the basis of 50 percent of the operational costs provided by the Department of Corrections, having 50 percent of the bed space; the county would pay the other 50 percent of operating costs and have 50 percent of the bed space. Local officials doubted the long-term financial viability of such an arrangement and were concerned about who would make the decisions about the release of felons back into the community. County officials would have felt more confidence in the provisions of Senate Bill 2000 if they had a right to veto decisions by the Department of Corrections about the release of felons from these proposed community correctional centers.

A Californian district attorney took the following view of the advantage of having secure local residential facilities:

> A community corrections program needs to develop some kind of confined setting because you are talking about felons with serious records that should not be directly out on the street in contact with the public. These individuals have been through the system many times and generally have been on probation one, two, three, four times and it hasn't worked. Supervision, even intensive supervision, won't work. For the purposes of accountability and punishment, there has got to be something at the local level that the court can use to house these people. (Davies, 1990)

Continuity of Monitoring

In recent years, more effective means of surveillance in community settings have been developed (e.g., 24-hour reporting systems, electronically monitored home confinement, intensive supervision). Sentencers and correctional officials may have been tempted to see custody as the only means of achieving appropriate control over, and supervision of, offenders. Where surveillance is required, but not at the level requiring incarceration, and not at the same cost, intermediate sanctions can be regarded as a more effective use of criminal justice resources.

A chief probation officer describes the extent of surveillance and the sanctions for failure in the case of intensive supervision:

> The possibility that someone gets probation and nobody worries about them is not the case with intensive supervision. They are watched seven days a week, 18 hours a day in this county. If they violate this probation, it goes back to the court; and nine times out of ten, that individual is on his way to the state penitentiary or county jail. (Davies, 1991, p 9)

The degree of surveillance would depend on the offenders and their assessed risk. The array of programs would have to be related to offender needs. Programs would involve the delivery of services to offenders. Funding costs could match and surpass incarceration costs if the comprehensive range of services identified by the panelists were made available to all offenders. For the rehabilitative element, there must be a comprehensive and wide range of service providers, so that offenders with multiple problems can be helped in a way that is likely to achieve life-style changes. This cannot be done in a piecemeal fashion.

Furthermore, behavior modification is not likely to be easy. Along with a low-success criteria goes the need to provide long-term follow-up with services and counseling. Officials believed that past rehabilitative programs were unsuccessful because it was easy for an offender to get lost in the system. The system processes the arrestee-offender-inmate through many stages. So in addition to a long-term strategy of behavior modification, greater continuity of supervision is required as the offender proceeds through the system. Continuity is a key quality if intermediate sanctions are to succeed as a multipurpose and multidimensional form of punishment.

CRIMINAL JUSTICE OFFICIALS' VIEWS ON INTERMEDIATE SANCTIONS

California, as elsewhere, is under increasing fiscal pressure to introduce a Community Corrections Act. In the summer of 1990 in California, I used focus groups to ask seventy-three senior criminal justice officials what they thought was the major issue to be resolved before there could be an expanded role for intermediate sanctions.

Reflecting the Blue Ribbon Commission members' concern with a more "balanced" and "systematic" approach, the panelists suggested that the multiple goals of the system can each contribute in such a way as to maintain public and professional confidence in the system. A credible system of intermediate sanctions should provide a composite form of sentence with multiple goals for intermediate offenses.

Any impression of a swing in the pendulum between "soft" and "tough" sentencing should be avoided. The introduction of determinate sentencing in 1976 and the subsequent expansion of the use of imprisonment has not proved to be any more successful in allaying public anxiety about crime than the previous system with its considerable emphasis on offender rehabilitation.

As the sentence received by 66 percent of all convicted felons involved some form of intermediate sanctions, the existence of community-based, intermediate sanctions was widely accepted. It was evident that with limited financial resources some counties were closing down services and reducing the use of others because of a lack of funding, especially for the more expensive residential programs involving drug therapy. Those on routine probation, usually after a short jail sentence, will be, in effect, unsupervised. This worried most panelists, but the "bottom line," as several pointed out, was funding.

Much of the debate on intermediate sanctions has taken place in the context of the overcrowding in prisons and jails and the spiraling costs of incarceration. The "bottom-liners" see this as the only reality. Emphasis on the economics of punishment and the expediency of reducing costs is likely to lead to cynicism and a lack of direction, as this comment from a county director of corrections suggested:

> The pendulum is beginning to swing the other way, not driven by altruistic views about rehabilitation or what is most appropriate, but rather it's cost driven. . . . the goal seems to be to reduce cost, not to improve effectiveness. I think the criminal justice system statewide, through the legislature, needs to get clear what it is trying to do, what are our goals, and set performance objectives that are not driven strictly by dollars. (Davies, 1991, p. 6)

If we refine our bottom line question so that it asks not just "What does it cost?" but "Does what we spend give us value for our money?" we need to know what it is we should be evaluating (i.e., what are the penological objectives of intermediate sanctions other than reducing prison overcrowding and keeping down costs).

The predominant view of the panelists about the purposes of intermediate sanctions was that they should be multipurposed. If intermediate sanctions are to be effective and acceptable so that the public has confidence in them in a denunciatory-retributive sense, then most of the panelists seemed to think that they must combine the characteristics of punishment, surveillance and rehabilitation. That is, they should be recognized as a seeking to achieve multiple purposes. If rehabilitation does not succeed, and most officials in California expect and predict a low rehabilitative success rate, then the punitive element will have served denunciatory purposes, and the surveillance element given some assurances that the offender who is released back into the community will be monitored to some degree.

A number of panelists accepted a rehabilitative logic in which the purpose of the system was to change behavior; they viewed prisons as expensive and counterproductive. For these officials resources would be better spent on programs both in institutions and also in the community.

A sheriff pointed out that most felons already come from, and stay in, the community, "The fact is the people in our jails don't come from somewhere outside the area. They all come from our community, and we are going to turn them right back into the community. We at least should not turn them back worse off than when they came in" (Davies, 1991, p. 6). The Blue Ribbon Commission pointed out that with so many short-term felons and parole violators in prison soon returning to the community, public safety could be improved by holding them locally and subjecting them to life-style intervention programs.

The comments from the California panelists in the focus groups would suggest the following elements of a fully developed rehabilitative program: recognition of the low success criteria, long-term follow-up, multipurpose programming and comprehensive service provision, more flexibility and discretion in handling offenders on these programs, additional surveillance, and sanctions for failure.

Several panelists regarded the lack of flexibility at the sentencing and correctional stages as a consequence of the determinate sentencing laws. Some, like this chief assistant district attorney, expressed a view that they would like to see more discretion available with sentencing decisions. He said, "Right now you have a situation where everyone goes through like a herd of cattle, and there isn't any subjectivity in the process at all" (Davies, 1991, p. 10).

On what category of offender should we initially consider focusing intermediate sanctions? The correctional ocean is large in California. The Blue Ribbon Commission identifies the target population that would be eligible for community-based intermediate sanctions as follows:

A. California Department of Corrections Commitments
   1. Short-term new prison commitments serving one year or less, with emphasis on those serving six months or less
   2. Parole violators returned to prison with emphasis on those serving six months or less
B. California Youth Authority Commitments
   1. Some less serious non-violent offenders from juvenile courts
   2. Technical parole violators
   3. Offenders transitioning out of CYA (last 120 days)
C. Jail Commitments or Pre-Sentence Detainees
D. The community corrections target population specified above should be further limited to non-violent property offenders, including drug abusers, with emphasis on first-time offenders and those without a significant criminal history (Blue Ribbon Commission, p. 114–5)

The above categories from the report used to identify inmate eligibility for intermediate sanctions were accepted by most panelists. What concerned them most was screening the eligible population in terms of risks and needs of offenders, and who would be in control of screening, the state or the county? The target population for intermediate sanctions has been identified by most theorists and policy documents as prison-bound offenders. In the American Correctional Association's model for a community corrections act, the first of eight components identifies "a clearly defined target group of prison-bound offenders" (McManus, 1978, p. 12).

Some panelists were concerned about the efficacy of dealing with felony inmates who had already reached prison and that it might be too late to do anything to change their behavior. One chief probation officer took the view:

> The problem is once they are at a level where they have to be committed to state prison, it is too late. They need state prison. If we put the resources when they were first involved in the commission of crimes so that we had them adjusted to the community and had whatever resources, whether it's drug rehab early in, we could prevent it. That's prevention. Eighty percent of the people going through felony hearings end up on probation now. If we would put a tenth of the money we put into state prison into making a real sanction or punishment when they first get probation, we might be able to make an impact. If you address the issue in the community, it has got to be early. It's too late once they need prison. (Davies, 1991, p. 7–8)

Given the target population of offenders, many of whom are repeat offenders and parole violators, some panelists doubted the likelihood of success with this group and thought money could be better spent on prevention for a younger target population and at-risk groups. Most accepted the view that with this target population of repeat felony offenders, the criteria for success in rehabilitative terms has to be low. Others, like this judge, thought rehabilitation should not be the primary concern of the sentence:

> My own personal feeling is that rehabilitation is a by-product of the system working appropriately. I don't think you focus in on rehabilitation. I think if you put someone in a situation where he is paying back the community for what he has done by work or whatever that allows him to get his dignity back. I think that comes from the process. Focusing in on taking this person and making him rehabilitated is never going to work. (Davies, 1991, p. 8)

This view about the credibility of rehabilitation was repeated when the focus group panels moved on to discuss probation and public confidence in rehabilitative goals. This led some panelists to a pessimistic attitude about the chances of extending intermediate sanctions into community settings. The comments of a county official reflect the view of others who have sympathy for more rehabilitative efforts with this group of inmates, but think they are unlikely to gain public support if they involve release into the community. He said, "I don't think it's going to be easy to sell intermediate sanctions in the community right now. It might be easier to bring the services to the inmates because I think the public still wants the inmates locked up" (p. 7).

A chief probation officer identified a similar public attitude, which applies equally to criminals and the criminal justice agencies:

> The biggest stumbling block to community-based sanctions is the local community resistance. People want to treat criminals like they treat their trash. They want to put it out by the curb and have someone come along to take it away. It is a very strong feeling in the community. I am trying to open up an office—not a facility—and the city is ready to sue me for moving into their city. It's just a probation office. (Davies, 1990, p. 16)

THE PUBLIC MOOD

Public acceptability is key to the success of intermediate sanctions. It becomes vital to assure the public that intermediate sanctions are only used when they are appropriate for individual offenders in the sense of being deserved and not because they are a cheaper option—part of a comprehensive framework of sentencing that is understood by the community and balances the needs of the offender against the needs of the community. But does the public have confidence in the existing community-based intermediate sanctions? Officials in California had their doubts: "The public is going to think that electronic surveillance or house arrest is a laugh. The public will never accept that as being a form of punishment. As far as being utilized, it's not really a form of punishment. It's a form of accountability and tracking" (Davies, 1991, p. 13).

"The public likes the idea that the inmate is working," said a judge (Davies, 1990, p. 16). Many of the panelists endorsed this view that the one form of intermediate sanction that had proved popular with the public were projects that involved public work in community settings, such as with the highway litter clearing gangs. The panelists thought the public confidence in this form of sanction increased because it combined an element of punitiveness with the idea of repaying the community, and the notion that work, in whatever form, might have some curative impact on the offender. There was more support for work-based intermediate sanctions than for the traditional forms of probation, which were regarded as misdirected, unsuccessful and no longer acceptable to the public.

A judge expressed his reservations about probation and described how he was likely in marginal sentencing decisions to prefer the use of prison:

> In our county, probation is underfunded, overworked, undermanned and so on. In the really close cases, I know they are not going to get anything from our probation system, so I ship them off to state prison. . . . I do not believe we have adequate supervision of our probationers. I am not knocking the probation department. They are doing an outstanding job, but the probation officer is being asked to oversee an unreasonable number of people. (Davies, 1991, p. 12)

With little public support for probation, a dramatic shift in role is envisioned by several chief probation officers in California. They have given up their individual welfare casework-oriented approach and are ready to subscribe to a more surveillance-oriented role, in which the casework, be it employment or social skills training, is handed over to specialist counselors in public or private practice. Except for the intensive supervision cases handled by probation, most probation work becomes a screening and monitoring role. The weight of numbers and the frustrations of failure have influenced this shift, along with the recognition of the declining public faith in probation as anything other than a token punishment. The chief probation officer of Los Angeles commented:

> Probation means more than half of the felons on probation are never seen. Probation right now means they go onto administrative caseloads and are never seen. They are tracked only by computer. That's what it means. The other half get supervised in caseloads of between 35 to 200. A lot of the felons that end up on probation should not be on probation. They need to be incarcerated . . .
>
> I believe the probation officers should only provide the surveillance and the sanction. I don't believe probation officers should do the treatment or counselling. I believe there are specialists who are trained to do that. If I have the resources, I could provide the kind of supervision so that I knew what the probationers were doing. That's why I would want my resources doubled. The other resources would be to go to private or public agencies who are trained to do specifically drug counselling, job counselling, and all that. I don't believe the probation officer can be the counsellor to everyone . . .
>
> Many probation officers across the country are no longer calling themselves probation departments. They are becoming community corrections agencies or community safety agencies. They are no longer called probation. The public will never get over the perception that probation is "getting off." (Davies, 1991, p. 11)

When dealing with a caseload of serious and persistent offenders, as would be the situation if sanctions are extended to a wider range of offenders, monitoring becomes vital in assuring the public that they are being protected. A chief probation officer argues the need for greater emphasis on prevention and supervision:

> An effective system in my view has to invest in preventing the circumstances and situations that result in crime. Not to incarcerate someone after they have earned their ticket, but to prevent that crime from occurring that earns them the ticket. We haven't done a very good job. In fact, we have done worse and worse. All of the community-based corrections programs and non-institutional programs have gotten worse. We have 257,000 people in California that are out there on the streets that are convicted, on probation and supervised zilch. (Davies, 1991, p. 11)

This same chief probation officer recognized that probation has a problem of public credibility. "Probation has a very negative connotation. We don't know what to call ourselves anymore. We haven't come up with anything any better than what we have. Corrections also does not have a very good taste in your mouth with the general public. Probation is even worse" (Davies, 1991, p. 11). The general public's view of probation as "getting off" is confirmed by a judge, "The public perception when I put somebody on probation, is that the judge has given this person a break" (Davies, 1991, p. 12).

Are public officials, judges or politicians good at assessing the public mood on sentencing? Was the Californian judge correct to assume that the public regard probation as getting off lightly? Mike Hough (1987) wrote, "In Britain, it is probably fair to say that practitioners and politicians alike are pessimistic, and assume widespread public dissatisfaction with the perceived leniency of the courts" (p. 1). In the United States, Gottfredson, Warner, and Taylor (1988), in their interviews with 80 correctional policy makers and telephone survey of 600 residents of Maryland, came to the conclusion that, "Contrary to general belief, we found the general public not to be especially punitive," and their utilitarian goals for corrections were shared by the penal policy makers. However, the policy makers assume "that the public's attitudes concerning correctional issues is at substantial variance with their own" (p. 45).

But in California the Field Institute on March 28, 1990 published the results of its telephone sample of 500 Californians to show that 84 percent agreed with the statement that "criminals should be punished harshly to demonstrate that society cares about the victims of crime." But 56 percent disagreed with the statement that "it is more important that prisons punish criminals than rehabilitate them." Part of the explanation of the variations in these findings might be accounted for by geographic or cultural differences in outlook, the methodology employed, or the reflection of public support for both goals. The public recognize that there is more than one aim of the criminal justice system. How they come to make judgments about those aims will depend on their level of knowledge about events, the information they are given when asked a question, the contextual influence of high profile cases, the criteria they use in response to questions, and their own personal experience of crime.

The findings of the British Crime Survey indicated the public's ambiguity about sentencing practice. According to Hough and Mayhew (1985), "Certainly the findings are at odds with the impression which public opinion polls tend to give of a thoroughly punitive public. If people are asked at a general level whether court sentences are adequate, a great majority answer that they are not. But if they are asked—as in the British Crime Survey—about a specific incident involving themselves, and thus have a concrete example upon which to base their judgements, they are less punitive" (p. 28).

Clearly, there are a number of problems in assessing public attitudes to sentencing in general. Thomson and Ragona (1987) caution against building policy decisions based on opinion polls. They note, "There is a lack of specificity with respect to the types of cases and offenders they are asked to judge. This lack of specificity in conjunction with the global nature of questions asked suggests that respondents may be reacting to boundary-defining images that have been formed by media accounts of particularly heinous, and hence unrepresentative offenses" (p. 340).

If there is a problem of interpreting data about punishment in general, is there more useful data on public attitudes about the use of intermediate sanctions? Hough and Mayhew (1985) found evidence in the British Crime Survey that there is "considerable tolerance for alternatives to imprisonment amongst the general public" (p. 46). However, an international comparison published by Kluwer Law and Taxation Publishers (1990) showed that only a third of U.K. residents favored a community service order for a recidivist burglar aged twenty-one, compared with 53 percent in favor in the United States and 60 percent in Germany. Across the United States, *The Figgie Report* (1985) found, in a 1984 survey on the public's views as to how to solve prison overcrowding, that 75 percent of respondents wanted more prisons built and 67 percent wanted more offenders diverted into alternative programs. Clearly, these are not mutually exclusive solutions.

There seems to be an absence of detailed investigations about the acceptability of community-based intermediate sanctions in the United Kingdom and the United States. Jeffrey Senese (1990), writing about a facet of intermediate sanctions—intensive supervision programs—stated, "One aspect of contemporary intensive supervision programs which appears to have escaped study has been public perceptions of its appropriateness" (p. 7). His research in Indiana is based on a telephone sample of 200. He finds that "intensive supervision probation is most favored for those who commit minor theft. The respondents also are of the opinion that intensive supervision can be used with major theft (53 percent), burglary (34 percent), driving under the influence (41 percent), and drug abuse (47 percent). Although the proportions of respondents that believe that intensive supervision sentences are appropriate for violent offenses are relatively low, they are much higher than one might expect [5 percent]" (p. 15).

In 1987 a telephone survey conducted by Bowling Green State University of 1,920 adults found that in response to eight crime vignettes, covering a range of serious criminal offenses, the majority (71 percent) chose incarceration over community sanctions. In reply to this survey, Barry Krisberg (1988) stated, "Asking people who are generally uninformed very specific policy questions may reveal their state of ignorance, but their responses could hardly be taken seriously as the basis for policy-making." I think that public opinion has to be taken into account in a democracy, if there is to be public confidence in the criminal justice system.

But raw public opinion should not be used as a simplistic way to reach policy decisions. More subtle means of evincing public concerns about crime and punishment are required. According to Krisberg, "The focus group approach often produces more complex and subtle mapping of public opinion than the telephone survey" (p. 3). The Public Agenda Foundation report by John Doble (1987) provides a good example of this. In 1986 ten locations across the United States were used to hold focus group panels to discuss attitudes about crime and punishment. Doble's panels of citizens shared the view held by the Californian panelists that a low rehabilitative success rate is to be expected, but they had more support for the goal of rehabilitation than the Californian officials had anticipated.

Doble's panels of citizens were supportive of the idea of a "cocktail" of multifaceted and comprehensive community sanctions. Doble wrote, "Respondents also felt that a combination of alternatives could be employed simultaneously. For example, many felt that mandatory drug abuse treatment, intensive or enriched probation, and halfway houses could be used together with other alternatives" (p. 36).

What is certain is that whatever the detailed form taken by intermediate sanctions, public and professional credibility is a vital ingredient for its success. How can policy makers improve their understanding of what the public wants from its criminal justice system without reducing policy formulation to whimsical and faddish populism? Through appropriate forms of public and professional consultation, policy makers can improve the correspondence between policy aspirations and public expectations. One way to do this is through the use of focus groups as a means of reducing the likelihood of sentencing and penal reforms succumbing to the utopianism of penal reformers who pursue goals regardless of public and professional opinion.

Can the process of public consultation be improved? How is the ocean of public concern and opinion to be articulated? There should be some correspondence between the sensibilities and vision of the sentencers and public. But direct public control over sentencing policy should be avoided. Jock Young (1991) wrote, "Social surveys can, therefore, provide us with a democratic input into the direction and prioritization of crime control. But they cannot provide us with a blueprint. You cannot read policy directives from social surveys but neither can you provide directives without a real consumer input" (p. 49).

The first step is to improve our understanding of consumer needs, and "if any weight is to be attached to public opinion in sentencing, then the contours of this opinion must be mapped more fully, more systematically and more dispassionately than is done at present" (Hough and Lewis, 1986, p. 8).

Start with the public concerns and sense of priorities; improve the sophistication of the mode of assessing public opinions through the use of focus groups; promote public understanding of the system; and recognize that filters are required between the public's subjective concerns and sensibilities and the determination and responsibilities of sentencing policy. Filters are required for two paramount reasons. First, knowledge and expertise are required to understand and balance the competing legal, administrative and resource implications of penal decisions. Second, although public attitudes should provide part of the evaluation of the seriousness of the offense and the appropriateness of the sentencing tariff in general terms, the tariff must not succumb to ad hoc political lobbying. Rather, it should offer a framework of sentencing with consideration given to principles of proportionality, fairness and certainty.

References

Babie, E. 1973. *Survey Research Methods*. Belmont: Wadsworth.

Barnes, H. E. 1930. *The Story of Punishment: The Story of Man's Inhumanity to Man*, 2nd edition, 1972. Montclair, N.J.: Patterson Smith.

Blue Ribbon Commission. 1990. *Report on Inmate Population Management*. January. Sacramento: Department of Corrections.

Blumberg, A. S. 1967. *Criminal Justice*. Chicago: Quadrangle Books.

Bowling Green State University. 1987. Survey results in J. Jacoby and C. Dunn, eds., *National Survey on Punishment for Criminal Offenses*. Washington: U.S. Bureau of Justice Statistics.

Braithwaite, J. 1989. *Crime, Shame and Reintegration*. Cambridge: Cambridge University Press.

Braithwaite, J., and P. Pettit. 1990. *Not Just Deserts: A Republican Theory of Criminal Law*. Oxford: Clarendon Press.

Boyd, W. 1982. *An Ice-Cream War*. London: Hamish Hamilton.

Brittan, A. 1981. "The Symbolic Dimension of Law and Social Control," in A. Podgorecki and C. Whelan, eds., *Sociological Approaches to Law*, pp. 167–187. London: Croom Helm.

Bureau of Criminal Statistics 1987. *Crime and Delinquency in California, 1986*. Sacramento: Department of Justice.

———. 1990. *Crime and Delinquency in California, 1980–1989*. Sacramento: Department of Justice.

California Supreme Court. 1918. Quoted from a Supreme Court decision *in re Lee*, 1918.

Canadian Law Reform Commission. 1976. *Our Criminal Law*. Report of the Canadian Law Reform Commission, Ottawa.

Cohen, A. 1985. *The Symbolic Construction of Community*. Tavistock: London.

Cohen, S. 1985. *Visions of Social Control: Crime, Punishment and Classification.* Cambridge: Polity.

Cullen, F., Cullen, J., and J. Wozniak. 1988. "Is Rehabilitation Dead? The Myth of the Punitive Public," *Journal of Criminal Justice* vol. 16, pp. 303–317.

Davies, M. 1985. "Determinate Sentencing Reform in California and Its Impact on the Penal System," *British Journal of Criminology* vol. 25, no. 1, pp. 1–30.

———. 1988a. *Survey Report: The Expansion of the Criminal Justice System and Penal System in California—Is Greater Coordination Required?* Bureau of Criminal Statistics Monograph Series. Sacramento: Office of the Attorney General, California Department of Justice.

———. 1988b. *Coordinating Justice in California: There Ought to Be a Law About It.* Bureau of Criminal Statistics Forum Series. Sacramento: Office of the Attorney General, California Department of Justice.

———. 1989. "Square Deal Punishment in the Community: It Is Cheaper But Who Will Buy It?" in H. Rees and E. Hall Williams, eds., *Punishment, Custody and the Community: Reflections and Comments on the Green Paper*, pp. 19–33, London: Suntory Toyota International Centre for Economics and Related Disciplines, London School of Economics.

———. 1990. *Community Corrections—A Swing of the Pendulum?* Report presented to the Special Legislative Hearing on "State and Local Partnership on Criminal Justice," December 5, 1990, Sacramento. Guggenheim Criminal Justice Series. Berkeley: Guggenheim Criminal Justice Program.

———. 1991. *A Policy Role for Focus Groups: Community Corrections.* Bureau of Criminal Statistics Forum Series. Sacramento: California Department of Justice.

Department of Corrections. 1988. *Mission and Philosophy Document Statement and Department Priorities*. Sacramento: Department of Corrections.

———. 1992. *CDC Facts*. July 1, 1992. Sacramento: Department of Corrections.

Deukmejian, G. 1987. A covering letter was written by the Governor at the time he formally approved Senate Bill no. 279 establishing the Blue Ribbon Commission. Sacramento: Capitol.

———. 1988. "The Governors State of the State Address," *Los Angeles Times*, January 7, 1988, p. 18.

DiIulio, J. 1987. *Governing Prisons*. New York: Free Press.

Doble, J. 1987. *Crime and Punishment: The Public's View*. New York: Public Agenda Foundation.

Embert, P., and D. Kalinch, 1988. *Behind the Walls*, Module Z. Salem, Wis.: Sheffield Publishing.

Feeley, M. 1983. *Court Reform on Trial: Why Simple Solutions Fail*. New York: Basic Books.

Feinberg, J. 1965. "The Expressive Function of Punishment," *The Monist* vol. 49, no. 3, pp. 397–423.

Field Institute. 1990. "Public Opinion Poll Report on Punishment," by C. Zukin and M. DiCamillo, press release of the Field Institute, March 28, 1990. San Francisco: Field Institute.

Figgie Report. 1985. *The Figgie Report Part V: Parole—Search for Justice and Safety*. Richmond, Va.: Figgie International.

Foucault, M. 1977. *Discipline and Punish: The Birth of the Prison*. London: Allen Lane.

Garland, D. 1985. *Punishment and Welfare: A History of Penal Strategies*. Aldershot, England: Gower.

———. 1989 "Critical Reflections on the Green Paper," in H. Rees and E. Hall Williams, eds., *Punishment, Custody and the Community: Reflections and Comments on the Green Paper*, pp. 4–18, London: Suntory Toyota International Centre for Economics and Related Disciplines, London School of Economics.

———. 1990. "Frameworks of Inquiry in the Sociology of Punishment," *British Journal of Sociology* vol. 41, no. 1, pp. 1–15.

Gordon, R. 1990. *The Justice Juggernaut*. New Brunswick, N.J.: Rutgers University Press.

Gottfredson, S., Warner B., and R. Taylor. 1988. "Conflict and Consensus in Justice System Decisions," in N. Walker and M. Hough, eds., *Public Attitudes Towards Sentencing: Surveys from Five Countries*. Aldershot: Gower.

Gottfredson, M., and T. Hirschi. 1990. *A General Theory of Crime*. Stanford, Calif.: Stanford University Press.

Gross, H. 1979. *A Theory of Criminal Justice*. New York: Oxford University Press.

Hart, H.L.A. 1968. *Punishment and Responsibility*. Oxford: Clarendon Press.

Hibbert, C. 1978. *The Roots of Evil: Social History of Crime and Punishment*. London: Greenwood Press.

Home Office. 1959. *Penal Practice in a Changing Society*. London: HMSO.

———. 1990. *Crime, Justice and Protecting the Public*. Cm. 965, London: HMSO.

Hough, M., and P. Mayhew. 1985. *Taking Account of Crime: Key Findings from the 1984 British Crime Survey*. Home Office Research Study No. 85. London: HMSO.

Hough, M., and H. Lewis. 1986. "Penal Hawks and Penal Doves: Attitudes to Punishment in the British Crime Survey," *Research Bulletin*, no. 21. Home Office Research and Planning Unit. London: HMSO.

Hough, M. 1987. "Attitudes to Punishment in England and Wales: Some Survey Findings." Paper presented at the National Conference on Punishment, Ann Arbor, Mich., November.

Hutchinson, Lord, Q. C. 1988. "Prisoners of Supply and Demand," *The Times* [London] November, 1988, p. 40.

Irwin, J., and J. Austin. 1987. *It's About Time: Solving America's Prison Crowding Crisis*. San Francisco: National Council on Crime and Delinquency.

Jacques, M. 1990. "A Glass of Red Wine Mr. Marx?" *Financial Times* [London] March 10, 1990, p. B1.

Judicial Council of California. 1987. *Annual Report of the Judicial Council 1987*. San Francisco: Administrative Office of the Courts.

Kluwer Law and Taxation Publishers. 1990. *Experiences of Crime Across the World: Key Findings of the 1989 International Crime Survey*. Deventerm, Holland: Kluwer.

Krisberg, B. 1988. "Public Attitudes about Criminal Sanctions," *Facts*, January 27, 1988. San Francisco: National Council on Crime and Delinquency.

Krueger, R. A. 1988. *Focus Groups: A Practical Guide for Applied Research.* Beverly Hills: Sage.

Larivee, J. 1990. "Day Reporting Centers: Making Their Way From the UK to the USA," *Corrections Today* October, pp. 84–89.

Lewis, C. S. 1953. "On Punishment," *Res Judicatae* vol. 6, 1952–1954.

Luririo, A., ed. 1990. *Crime and Delinquency Special Issue: Intensive Probation Supervision: An Alternative to Prison in the 1990s* vol. 36, no. 1, January.

Mathiesen, T. 1990. *Prison on Trial: A Critical Assessment.* London: Sage.

McMahon, M. 1990. "Net-Widening: Vagaries in the Use of a Concept," *British Journal of Criminology* vol. 30, No. 2, Spring, pp. 121–149.

McManus, P., and L. Barclay. 1978. *Community Corrections Act: Technical Assistance Manual.* College Park, Maryland: American Correctional Association.

Merton, R. K. 1978. "The Focused Interview and Focus Groups; Continuities and Discontinuities," *Public Opinion Quarterly* vol. 51, pp. 550–566.

Messinger, S., and J. Berecochea. 1990. *Don't Stay Too Long But Do Come Back Soon: Reflections on the Size and Vicissitudes of California's Prisoner Population.* Paper given at the Berkeley Conference on Growth and Its Influences on Correctional Policy; Perspectives on the Report of the Blue Ribbon Commission, May 10–11, 1990.

Messinger, S., Berecochea, J., Berk, R., and D. Rauma. 1988. *Parolees Returned to Prison and the California Prison Population.* Bureau of Criminal Statistics Collaborative Report with the University of California, Sacramento: California Department of Justice.

Morris, N., and M. Tonry. 1990. *Between Prison and Probation: Intermediate Punishment in a Rational Sentencing System.* New York: Oxford University Press.

Nagel, I. 1990. "Sentencing Discretion: The New Federal Sentencing Guidelines," *Journal of Criminal Law and Criminology*, vol. 80, no. 4, pp. 883–943.

National Association for the Care and Resettlement of Offenders [NACRO]. 1991. *Nacro News*, no. 3, London: NACRO.

National Institute of Justice. 1990. *The Use of Electronic Monitoring by Criminal Justice Agencies, 1989*. Washington: National Institute of Justice.

Ohlin, L., and F. Remington. 1958. "Sentencing Structure; Its Effects upon Systems for the Administration of Criminal Justice," *Law and Contemporary Problems* vol. 23, pp. 495–507.

Patten, J. 1991. *The Times* [London] February 5th, 1991, p. 32.

Petersilia, J. 1987. *Expanding Options for Criminal Sentencing*. Santa Monica, Calif.: Rand.

———. 1990. "When Probation Becomes More Dreaded Than Probation," *Federal Probation* vol. 54, no. 1, pp. 23–27.

Piachaud, D. 1991. "Revitalizing Social Policy," *Political Quarterly* vol. 62, no. 2, pp. 204–224.

Presley, R. Senator. 1983. *Sentencing Guidelines Commission*. Summary report of a seminar held on March 21, 1983. Sacramento: Capitol.

Primoratz, I. 1989. *Justifying Legal Punishment*. Atlantic Heights, N.J.: Humanities Press.

Rasmussen, J. 1991. These comments were made in a letter written to the author, March 20, 1991.

Richardson, J. 1988. "Prison Guards Emerge as a Major Lobbying Force," *Sacramento Bee*, March 22, 1988, p. 24.

Roberts, J. 1990. Report by Quentin Cowdry in *The Times* [London] October 26, 1990, p. 3.

Scull, A. 1977. *Decarceration: Community Treatment and the Deviant*. Englewood Cliffs, N.J.: Prentice Hall.

Senese, J. 1990. "Intensive Supervision Probation and Public Opinion: Who Cares One Way or the Other?" Paper presented at the American Society of Criminology Conference, Baltimore, November 8, 1990.

Silbey, S. 1989. "A Sociological Interpretation of the Relationship between Law and Society," in R. Neuhas, eds., *Law and the Ordering of Our Life Together*. Grand Rapids, Mich.: Eerdmans.

Skolnick, J. 1974. *Justice Without Trial*. New York: John Wiley.

Smart, V. 1988. "Curfew Plans to Cut Jail Sentences," *Sunday Observer* [London], April 24, 1988, p. 2.

Stewart, D., and P. Shamdasani. 1990. *Focus Groups: Theory and Practice*. Newbury Park, Calif.: Sage.

Tawney, R. H. 1938. *Religion and the Rise of Capitalism.* London: Penguin Books.

Thomson, D., and A. Ragona. 1987. "Popular Moderation versus Governmental Authoritarianism: An Interactionist View of Public Sentiments Toward Criminal Sanctions," *Crime and Delinquency* vol. 33, no. 2, pp. 337–357.

Tonry, M. 1987. *Sentencing Reform Impacts.* National Institute of Justice, Washington: Department of Justice.

Tumim, S. 1991. *Independent* [London] February 26, 1991, p. 21.

United States Department of Justice. 1990. *Bureau of Justice Statistics Annual Report.* Washington: Department of Justice.

Vass, A. 1990. *Alternatives to Custody: Punishment, Custody and the Community.* London: Sage.

Waddington, P. 1991. "Book Review of Gordon's *The Justice Juggernaut,*" *British Journal of Criminology* vol. 31, no. 3, Summer, p. 323.

Walker, N., and C. Marsh. 1984. "Do Sentences Affect Public Disapproval?" *British Journal of Criminology* vol. 24, no. 1, pp. 27–48.

Walker, N. 1985. *Sentencing: Theory, Law and Practice.* London: Butterworths.

Walker, N. and M. Hough. 1988. *Public Attitudes to Sentencing: Surveys in Five Countries.* London: Gower.

Walker, R., ed. 1985. *Applied Qualitative Research.* Aldershot, England: Gower.

Walters, D. 1988. *Sacramento Bee*, May 10, 1988, p. 3.

Woolf Report. 1990. *Prison Disturbances in 1990.* Cmnd.1415 London: Home Office.

Young, J. 1991. "Ten Principles of Realism," Paper given at the British Criminology Conference, University of York, 1990, p. 49.

Index

About the Author

MALCOLM DAVIES, Professor of Psychology in the Law School, Thames Valley University in London, has published a number of studies dealing with intermediate sanctions. He was a Senior Research Fellow in the Bureau of Criminal Statistics in California's Attorney General's Office and a Visiting Scholar at the University of California at Davis Law School and at the Center for the Study of Law and Society, Berkeley.